NO CARROT

Just the Zen of it

*Talks and discussions
with*

David Ferguson

By the Same Author

THE WISDOM OF DAVID: VOLUME 1
THE WISDOM OF DAVID: VOLUME 2

Cassette recordings of David Ferguson's live discourses are available from:

>   THE FOUNDATION
>   P.O.BOX 39
>   HONITON
>   DEVON
>   EX 14 9YN

*To Rosemary in the hossen we share,
and to all my friends who come to Peacefields,
without whom this work would never have taken place.*

Copyright David Ferguson 2001
British Library Cataloguing in Publication Data
A catalogue record for this book is available from the British Library

Published in the United Kingdom 2001 by
The Foundation
P.O. Box 39
Honiton
Devon
EX14 9YN

All rights reserved: no part of this book may be reproduced or utilised in any form whatsoever, electronic or mechanical, or transmitted or stored in a retrieval system, in any form or by any means, without permission in writing from The Foundation.

Printed in the U.K.

ISBN 0 9526154 2 8

Acknowledgements

I wish to especially thank Devopama for encouraging me to produce this collection of my dialogues, prodding me along whenever necessary, and to acknowledge all his work in compiling and editing the spoken word into a presentable written form. I also wish to thank Lyn for so patiently transcribing the tapes, and Lyn and Sally for one morning brilliantly suggesting the title. Thanks are also due to Asho for her early assistance in the task of transcription; to Ivor for his computer skills in producing the initial drafts; to Robert for providing the recording equipment; to Phil for designing the cover and his professional help in seeing the text through publishing; and to my partner, Rosemary, for all her love and support.

CONTENTS

Acknowledgements	v
Preface	ix
The Great Way	1
Introduction - Mysticism	7
Truth	10
A Conversation	12
The Taoist Stallholder	34
Meditation	35
Timelessness	50
Motivation	51
Desire	54
Survival	55
The Having Mode and Existential Being	58
Freedom	59
The Nature of Opposites	66
Identity	72
Kensho	82
The Unsayable: Hossen	83
Discourses from a Retreat at Sennen:	
Tuesday	96
Wednesday	107
Thursday	114
Friday	120
Saturday	125
Zen	131

Preface

The talks and discussions recorded here took place over the last two years, and it must always be remembered that this work is fluid, changing. There is no final statement, true for a supposed eternity. David, like mystics down the centuries, is trying to express what can only be hinted at, glimpsed. In the wisdom of Lao Tzu, "The Tao is forever undefined. When you have names and forms, know that they are provisional."

David holds seven-day retreats at a small Centre in the Southwest of England and in the Austrian Alps. The seven days are structured around an hour's sitting meditation before breakfast, then a morning discourse with time for questions at the end. This is followed by a silent period until everyone comes together for the evening meal. During the afternoons David sees participants individually for an hour each at a time. After dinner there is a round-the-table open discussion, and a shorter sitting meditation before bed. The cumulative effect of the meditations together, the talks and discussions, the silent period, and the individual sessions is strong, profound often.

David also gives public talks in the Devon area, and there are classes with him twice a month for small groups of students who come regularly to his home at Peacefields.

THE GREAT WAY

*Verses on the Faith Mind
by Seng-ts'an
Third Zen Patriarch (606AD)*

The Great Way is not difficult
for those who have no preferences.
When love and hate are both absent
everything becomes clear and undisguised.
Make the smallest distinction, however,
and heaven and earth are set infinitely apart.
If you wish to see the truth
then hold no opinions for or against anything.
To set up what you like against what you dislike
is the disease of the mind.
When the deep meaning of things is not understood
the mind's essential peace is disturbed to no avail.

★ ★ ★

The Way is perfect like vast space
where nothing is lacking and nothing is in excess.
Indeed, it is due to our choosing to accept or reject
that we do not see the true nature of things.
Live neither in entanglements of outer things
nor in inner feelings of emptiness.
Be serene in the oneness of things
and such erroneous views will disappear by themselves.
When you try to stop activity to achieve passivity
your very effort fills you with activity.
As long as you remain in one extreme or the other,
you will never know oneness.

★ ★ ★

Those who do not live in the single Way
fail in both activity and passivity,
assertion and denial.
To deny the reality of things
is to miss their reality;
to assert the emptiness of things
is to miss their reality.
The more you talk and think about it,
the further astray you wander from the truth.
Stop talking and thinking
and there is nothing you will not be able to know.
To return to the root is to find the meaning,
but to pursue appearances is to miss the source.
At the moment of inner enlightenment,
there is a going beyond appearance and emptiness.
The changes that appear to occur in the empty world
we call real only because of our ignorance.
Do not search for truth;
only cease to cherish opinions.

★ ★ ★

Do not remain in the dualistic state;
avoid such pursuits carefully.
If there is even a trace
of this and that, of right and wrong,
the mind essence will be lost in confusion.
Although all dualities come from the one,
do not be attached even to this one.
When the mind exists undisturbed in the Way,
nothing in the world can offend,
and when a thing can no longer offend,
it ceases to exist in the old way.

★ ★ ★

When no discriminating thoughts arise,
the old mind ceases to exist.
When thought objects vanish,

the thinking-subject vanishes,
and when the mind vanishes, objects vanish.
Things are objects because there is a subject or mind;
and the mind is a subject because there are objects.
Understand the relativity of these two
and the basic reality: the unity of emptiness.
In this emptiness the two are indistinguishable
and each contains in itself the whole world.
If you do not discriminate between coarse and fine
you will not be tempted to prejudice and opinion.

★ ★ ★

To live in the Great Way is neither easy nor difficult.
But those with limited views are fearful and irresolute;
the faster they hurry, the slower they go.
Clinging cannot be limited;
even to be attached to the idea of enlightenment
is to go astray.
Just let things be in their own way
and there will be neither coming nor going.

★ ★ ★

Obey the nature of things
and you will walk freely and undisturbed.
When thought is in bondage the truth is hidden,
for everything is murky and unclear.
The burdensome practice of judging
brings annoyance and weariness.
What benefit can be derived
from distinctions and separations?

★ ★ ★

If you wish to move in the One Way
do not dislike even the world of senses and ideas.
Indeed, to accept them fully
is identical with true enlightenment.
The wise man strives to no goals

but the foolish man fetters himself.
There is one Dharma, not many;
distinctions arise from the clinging needs of the ignorant.
To seek mind with discriminating mind
is the greatest of all mistakes.
Rest and unrest derive from illusion;
with enlightenment there is no liking and disliking.
All dualities come from ignorant inference.
They are like dreams or flowers in the air:
foolish to try and grasp them.
Gain or loss, right or wrong;
such thoughts must finally be abolished at once.

★ ★ ★

If the eye never sleeps,
all dreams will naturally cease.
If the mind makes no discriminations,
the ten thousand things
are as they are, of single essence.

★ ★ ★

To understand the mystery of this one-essence
is to be released from all entanglements.
When all things are seen equally,
the timeless self-essence is reached.
No comparisons or analogies are possible
in this causeless, relationless state.

★ ★ ★

Consider movement stationary
and the stationary in motion
and both movement and rest disappear.
When such dualities cease to exist
oneness itself cannot exist.
To this ultimate finality
no law or description applies.

★ ★ ★

For the unified mind in accord with the Way
all self-centred striving ceases.
Doubts and irresolutions vanish
and life in true faith is possible.
With a single stroke we are freed from bondage;
nothing clings to us and we hold to nothing.
All is empty, clear, self-illuminating,
with no exertion of the mind's power.
Here thought, feeling, knowledge, and imagination
are of no value.
In this world of suchness
there is neither self nor other-than-self.

★ ★ ★

To come directly into harmony with this reality
just simply say when doubt arises, "Not two".
In this "not two" nothing is separate,
nothing is excluded.
No matter when or where,
enlightenment means entering this truth.
And this truth is beyond extension
or diminution in time or space;
in it a single thought is ten thousand years.

★ ★ ★

Emptiness here, emptiness there,
but the infinite universe stands
always before your eyes.
Infinitely large and infinitely small;
no difference, for definitions have vanished
and no boundaries are seen.
So too with being and non-being.
Don't waste time in doubts and arguments
that have nothing to do with this.

★ ★ ★

One thing, all things;
move among and intermingle,
without distinction.
To live in this realisation
is to be without anxiety about non-perfection.
To live in this faith is the road to non-duality,
because the non-dual is one with the trusting mind.

★ ★ ★

Words!
The Way is beyond language,
for in it there is
no yesterday,
no tomorrow,
no today.

Introduction – Mysticism

To define mysticism as the ability to see the universe in a grain of sand doesn't answer, "Who is looking?" This is the question that zen confronts. As a mystic I experience self as not separate yet at the same time, paradoxically, I still feel separate in my life because that is the only way I can exist. So on the one hand it is like I am acting out of a state of separation and on the other hand the mystical experience seems to deny any such separation. It is this contradiction that we grow from in terms of our experience in mysticism.

If an eternal truth exists it is not something that is bound by the limit of my understanding. An absolute truth can only be the very process itself, and "I" am part of that same process. My mind can only seal truth into some parcel, if you like, of limitation, whereas any truth is so much bigger than that and inevitably will change and grow. I find that very exciting indeed.

We have the need to survive and if for one moment you can blow that need it means you are no longer demanding your own limitation of security. We are trying here to present a process of self-reflection that will engender in us our own investigative process and give a hint of the freedom that can exist there. That freedom isn't a concept, an idea. It is an experience of directness in the experience of life as it occurs from moment to moment. If the human brain can be free of the process of demanding its own survival, its demand of a limited identity, brain is then capable of being open to everything.

This experience is a totality, an absoluteness. It doesn't have form, shape or time, and it is almost devoid of dimension. The experience to the brain of that encounter seems to change the demand of "I" of its own survival. It frees it up, it doesn't allow it to restrict. The brain no longer demands a restriction in pursuance of a "me" surviving within that process. But this experience doesn't have a value in terms of my survival. It doesn't mean that I have achieved something. It doesn't have anything to offer me other than the experience of a freedom, which is beyond any demand.

Now I think that is the ultimate human challenge. It is bigger than any ideas that I might have about satori or nirvana because it realizes the relationship of brain to the universe. And it realises that if a God can be said to exist the human brain is its expression. That may be seen by some people as a heretical thing to say but to me it is a firm experience. I don't have a relationship with God, but I have a deep conviction in an intelligent order of survival. And within that experience I am able to say the human brain is how the universe experiences itself. Now why nature, God - God, nature, survival to me are inseparable - should want to do that I can't say because I am its process, I am not separate from it as its observer. Those that claim to be an observer, it seems to me, have fallen back into the trap of survival, attempting to survive outside of that process itself, and this you cannot.

The process of survival does not have any validity outside of the human mind, and for the human mind it is always a paradoxical situation. There is no way "I", if "I" am the process of experience, if "I" am the process of brain, if that is who "I" am, there is no way "I" can stand outside of that process. All we are then doing is trying to create an additional security for our own fears, we are not facing the reality.

The nearest I have come to an activity in human behaviour that has come close to this are the Zen Buddhists. In pointing to them, however, I am not talking of the theological belief systems surrounding Buddhism. But there are certain Zen Buddhists, it seems to me, that have approached this space with great awareness and great awakening, such as The Great Way of the Third Patriarch Seng-ts'an, what limited knowledge we have of him. I haven't as yet seen anyone else who has. I think the tendency is to fall into some philosophical resolution of the space we find ourselves in. To do this is so tempting that I can well understand why people do it. But to me that is really sowing the seeds of their own destruction in terms of their freedom and objectivity.

What's in it for me, says "I". But if I am free of the demand of what's in it for me, I can begin to get a completely different relationship with experience. I am totally free of the limitation my demand places on life. What then opens is wondrous and amazing. Suddenly there is a glimpse of reality beyond the separations we make of it. It's gone again but it is there just momentarily, almost as if the dimensions curled in on themselves. Something else exists, just in that moment. So, yes, the human brain can react to that experience momentarily.

What this book is attempting to do is to empower the individual into a self-reflective process that will break the ties of their own need for the security of survival. Everything I am saying in the book is by its nature a limitation. Yet if it can set about a reflective process that allows the reader to face the challenge here presented I think that would be an entirely new and very important step in mystical evolution. And it is a reflective process that will last you your lifetime.

Truth

"There is but one God, truth is his name."
(Guru Nanak)

I divide truth into two, the relative truth that the mind can have and absolute truth that is beyond mind. Mysticism is an awareness of absolute truth.

The nearest the mind can get to absolute truth is to acknowledge the experience that is encountered in life itself around us at any one moment, in everything we do, wherever we are. Truth is, and if that is the nearest we can get to it we have to acknowledge that truth is constantly changing, nothing is ever static. Everything is in movement, so truth itself is in movement. Truth is always new and has never happened before. The mind that believes it has is caught in the cycle of its own conditioning.

I think we have to let go of the idea that truth will have a value for us. Seeking it or not seeking it is not being open to truth, it is placing a limitation on it which it most certainly is not. Truth is everything - belief and non-belief. Truth is absolute, but when we divide it so that we can make a truth of it that our mind can have, then it becomes a relative value. We divide absolute and limit it into the beliefs that we hold, and all we find then is the limitation we have created - called enlightenment, for example.

Within all of us there is a point where we fight the demand that is being made because we reach that point of "self", that point of what we believe is truth. So subtle is this place that it can become a place where "self" hides, it becomes our separation and our identification, and so to find our own truth is to find our own "self". Confront your truth and you confront your "self"; self has nowhere else to run.

We have a choice to make, pursue your truth or be free of it. Belief in a truth is so secure, it allays the fear of death, it deals with the loss of self. Whereas freedom from a belief system offers the mind absolutely nothing and does nothing for your ego but confront it.

This freedom from any belief system is not a conceptual freedom, it is not an intellectual place. Rather it is an acknowledgement that the freedom of everything has no value to the mind. Self-realisation is the discovery that truth, "self", "I", you, are all divisions of absolute, limitations and separations of everything. To mind, something is truth; to being, everything is truth, God, whatever name you want to put on it. This is the paradox of duality, a koan that the mind cannot resolve. Realising the paradox cannot be resolved, the duality is confronted. At this point of acknowledgement the mind is no more. It is your choice whether to resolve the paradox into something called truth or to let go of the need to do that. Such letting go is the freedom I talk of.

It has no purpose this freedom, it has no truth, only the mind's reaction to the experience of life as it arises. Mind is experienced almost as a simple reaction to the universe, and an extra-dimensional relationship opens to mind. Freedom, joy, bliss, benediction, whatever you name it, is a reaction of mind that demands no truth of it. It is the freedom to demand no truth of it. Yet mind is still acknowledged for its beauty and perfection, for without that reaction "I" could not know I existed. That reaction gives me an identity that calls itself David.

The freedom I am talking of acknowledges the perfection of the experience and makes no limitation, makes no demand of it. Perfection does not lie in the mind's desires of experience. Experience is as it is. Mysticism is an acknowledgement of all that you are, what I call the clear mind that acknowledges the newness of change. Mysticism is the path of no preference, because it has no limitation and no separation.

A Conversation with David on his own 'spiritual' process

DEVO *David would you talk about how you came to this work?*

I think all my life I have tried very hard to find a purpose to it all. What is life, what does life mean, what are we doing here? I never was satisfied with the explanations given by the major theological beliefs. They don't really seem to me to have a foundation in a modern world, though I could see that they justified and consoled people's fears. But there was some part of me that constantly felt empty. I used to call it, for want of a better expression, a hole in my heart.

I set about trying to fill that hole. People would say to me that when I got older and when I got married it would all be different, but age and marriage did not fill that inner emptiness. Then people would say that when I had children it would be different, and I had two beautiful children and that still didn't make any difference. Then it was maybe about success and the trappings of success, so I changed my occupation and set about creating my own business, because prior to that I had worked in industry. I became moderately successful, and though never a really successful businessman certainly the business provided enough wherewithal to maintain a fairly high standard of living. And that still didn't really solve it.

I tried to search for some meaning in life in a theological sense. I searched the different belief systems of the world in an attempt to try and make sense of my feelings of inadequacy. I read all sorts of different things yet nothing seemed to fit the bill for me. There would be moments when someone would explain something like rebirth or reincarnation or karma and in some ways it made sense. I would try to build a belief system around that in an attempt to find an inner peace. But still nothing worked.

Then one day just walking down the street in a hurry I nearly knocked a little man flying. I am a fairly large person but he looked at me and apologised. I said, "No, it's my fault," whilst he insisted it was his. There was a gentleness about his attitude, his manner, his eyes, which I had never seen before. There wasn't any maliciousness, there was even no defence; it was just very open, very beautiful. It wasn't necessarily what was said, it was rather the difference in his response, the approach. Normally you hit somebody or bump into someone and it tends to be quite an aggressive experience, or maybe a very apologetic one. Whereas in this case it was neither. I had a chat with him and we began to meet regularly. He taught me about Vipassana. This incident changed the course of my life. It opened the doorway to my own investigation.

I suppose inevitably through life things go up and down. Like all business people I went through a very difficult period and my marriage came under strain as well. I became unwell and it culminated in me eventually having a nervous breakdown.

DEVO *Were you still with your Vipassana Teacher?*

No, this is post that period. I really think the Teacher didn't bring about my experiences. I believe what he did essentially was to give me criteria to work towards, give me the opportunity of self reflection and give me a method through Vipassana, though this often threw up for me more questions than it answered.

DEVO *And you had even done one or two Buddhist retreats?*

I'm not sure that is correct. What I would prefer to say is that I had done one or two retreats myself. I have always been very sceptical about direction in terms of self-reflection. To me the value of self-reflection lies in self-exploration. I think if you set about someone else's journey, however well meaning they are, inevitably you are limited by their ideas of it. I think you have to throw away the fear of your own inadequacy, and really take the bull by the horns and set about a process of failure or success based on your own investigation. I think that is important. You have got to learn the hard way, because even though someone else can tell you that such a way is right you may experience it to be wrong and discard it simply because you are looking at it completely differently, and vice versa of course. I believe that my role here, for example, is simply reflective, and if you can open the door to someone's own investigation that holds a greater value than actually what you say to them.

It seems to me that much of what I arrived at and the place I arrived at was the consequence of the environmental conditioning I was finding myself in, something which is true for everybody. The success or failure of my ambition for the journey in those days, I felt, was very much dependent on my own steerage, my own navigation. I ended up with Buddhism because to me it had a more functional, practical base. Buddhism was less concept and more self-practice and more self reflection. And that appealed to me because I have always felt that I was master of my own destiny. If I make a mess of things, it's me that has done so, and if I make a success of things then it's also me that's done so. I have always believed that, and I think that is reflected in Buddhism. So I followed the Buddhist course for quite a while.

DEVO *You weren't looking for a Guru, you weren't travelling to India, you weren't going to whatever teachers were around then?*

I think in hindsight that that was a very wise move. Originally I think it arose out of sheer obstinacy on my part. But looking back I think it was a very wise move because now when I'm working with people I can see how greatly a particular doctrine, teaching, way, mantra, whatever they have taken on, has restricted them. I never had that problem. I came to it with a very open mind and all I had was my own experience of life.

I have always argued that your own life experience is all you really need and nothing to date has changed my mind on that. The more restricted you become within an ideology or belief system or faith in what you are following it seems to me the further away you get from a true self reflection. You have got to try and stay as objective as you can with the whole process, and I am not sure you can do that if someone else is telling you what is right and what is wrong.

What started to emerge out of my nervous breakdown was a series of psychic phenomena that I could not ignore. Others seemed to believe they had value too. I quickly found myself with a group who were encouraging me to carry on this psychic work in an endeavour to find some value in it both for myself and for them. This channelling work was eventually called the channelings of Zed. It became quite internationally accepted as a sort of belief system, and I believe there are those in the world today who still follow quite closely these teachings, which they feel are of value to them. At the time I most certainly did because a lot of phenomena were happening there which I just couldn't understand.

Devo *And how did this channelling start?*

It just came out one day as a consequence of having a session with a local healer, a woman actually suggested to me by my doctor. As a consequence of that first session this phenomena started where I went into some peculiar trance. I would be completely unconscious. It would appear that in these trances my heart rate would double, I would sweat profusely, and this channelling would start. It grew to nearly seven hundred pages of recording over several years. My colleague at the time was the healer and she recorded all this down on paper and it became, I believe it still is to a certain degree, part of her understanding and her work.

The procedure was that we would sit once a week and I would go into trance, and then after the trance I would actually sit and hear what I had said. Up until that point I hadn't got a clue. At each trance there would be a selected number of people who would sit in on the group.

I had never really believed in such things, I had never believed they were possible. In fact the sceptical engineer within me originally was quite prepared to accept that this was some deep psychological problem which I had, for I would not say things I could not understand. I always seemed to have a comprehension of what was actually being said, so one could argue therefore that it could be the product of some subconscious nature of my own mind. But I could not explain away the clairvoyant nature of these psychic interpretations of life. If it was a psychological disorder how come it had a such a real clairvoyant quality?

DEVO *You were prophesying things that later became true?*

Indeed that was the case. There were hundreds of pages of this, and as I say it was very important for me and those around me at that time. What I can see in terms of what was happening then is that it was giving me a much broader perspective of the possibilities of life than I'd had before. It was broadening my mind into all sorts of areas of work which I wouldn't have given any credence to before. To a sceptical person like myself it was not acceptable there could be a whole additional world of movement outside of my own ken. But out of this experience I had to grow to accept that something did exist there.

DEVO *What sort of additional world?*

Like psychic work, like mystical work, like healing, a whole range of different subjects which I wouldn't even have given the time of day to before. I also began to realise that there was a lot of rubbish in this area too, a lot of emotional rubbish. I learnt that psychics are very lonely people who in some ways set about a process to be noticed within the social sphere they move in, and I don't think I was any exception.

So there could have been a vested interest in my own mental process to follow such a process. I believed implicitly at the time that I really had no control of it but clearly I did because when I eventually stopped doing it, it was I that decided to stop. There wasn't somebody up there who said this is it, there is nothing more to come through. So it was clearly within my own ambition and my own power to do it or not.

Now following that period I began to notice that my observation of the world was beginning to change. It was very little to start with, surreptitiously so, it wasn't based on some major movement, but things were starting to change. And I feel that could be for two reasons. I think the psychic work certainly helped because, as I have said, it broadened my restricted view of life. But secondly the type of objective training I had in Vipassana was also starting to enable me to see life in a much broader way. A physical interaction was beginning to happen on a much more expansive basis than I had ever experienced before.

Previously I had always only seen life from the narrow ambition that I had of it, in terms of my own survival, in terms of my own needs. Now I began to appreciate that a whole different picture was beginning to occur. A greater expansion in terms of hearing, touch, smell; everything was starting to expand. There were smells I hadn't smelt before, there were views of life I'd not seen before, not in a mystical sense you understand, rather in a practical way. But around the fringes of this there were phenomena that were also starting to occur that I could not explain. I would often interpret what someone was going to say before they said it. I would often be able to predict events long before they happened. It was almost like the time sphere of my life was beginning to change. Something else was happening which I wouldn't have believed in previously. It wasn't simply clairvoyance, there was a telepathic capability that seemed to be growing in my mind, which to a certain degree still exists. I don't give it much credence these days but I feel we have senses that we just don't use, and the Vipassana training had started to enhance those senses in a way that earlier I wouldn't have believed possible. The broadening went far beyond the simple physical nature of observation.

DEVO *By Vipassana training, do you mean the sitting, watching the breath, watching the thoughts passing through your mind?*

Observing the emotional states arising within me, both sitting and in life in general, and observing my relationship to the various things that are happening. Because to me it is not just about sitting, it is about life as a totality. And that had started in the early days. Even during the course of my post-nervous breakdown, even in my married days, there was a different observation, there was a different person emerging from what existed before. It was as if the transformation had taken place out of the nervous breakdown. Something psychologically had seemed to move in my head which had created a different relationship to life than had previously existed. Things that were important before no longer had much significance and things that were of no significance before now seemed to be of incredible importance.

Whereas before I would only see life very narrowly through my demand of it, now I was beginning to see there was a whole different feel to life, there was a whole value to life itself that was not my ambition of it. I think this is what Erich Fromm calls existential living as opposed to the having mode of grabbing things for yourself all the time. As the having mode disappeared within me existential living seemed to expand into a completely different place. I found value in life as it is, being present with it as it is, rather than in my ambition of it and in my ideas, beliefs and faiths of it. And as this happened the psychic sphere of my life was beginning to drop away. I began to see that the psychic work was simply a stepping stone for me to something that was much, much greater, the whole energy of existence, the whole of life itself. It was no longer restricted to some narrow interpretation.

I began to see there wasn't a right or wrong in life, there were just different views of life, views which were relative to the person's own conditioning and the environment in which they had grown up. If for example I had grown up in India I might well have been a Hindu, but as I'd grown up in England then it was as a Christian. It wasn't that Christianity was right or that Hinduism was right. Political beliefs also follow a similar sort of vein. It is simply that the conditioned interpretation of my own environment determines the attitude I follow.

In a way finding out there wasn't a rightness or wrongness about anything was a freeing thing. It was quite a transformation for me because most of my life up until then, politically and economically, had been based on the belief that there was a right way and it was simply a matter of finding it. I now began to realise that there wasn't a right way at all, that there was simply life. So the experience therefore began to become more important than the actual journey or destination I was setting about finding, more important than my various interpretations of it.

This opened the doors again and is really where I started on the road to mysticism. Mysticism sees that people from different religious backgrounds with different belief systems are quite perfect as they are and it has no ambition that they should be different. In a way that objectivity created for me a much clearer reflection of life, one not so limited. And that started the process within my own mind of trying to observe my relationship with myself in an existential way.

It was almost as if I was setting about building my own personal ladder, and as I was climbing this ladder all the things which I had held dear were beginning to fall away. It was like there is a tree of life and the main journey is actually to climb the trunk of the tree itself. You can walk along a branch but you do so at your peril. And this tree produced greater and greater self-reflection as I climbed it.

DEVO *By self-reflection you mean it was showing you your own conditioning and how that conditioning had formed a certain self?*

In a completely different way because up until that point I had always assumed that self-reflection was about actually seeing more of yourself. But out of the expansiveness that I talked about earlier came a self-reflection of what it really wasn't, all the things that I am that it isn't. I was discarding the narrow views that I had of life; they weren't holding any validity, they were beginning to fall away because I had lost the fear of losing them. They were all clustered in the past for me, and they were there because of the need I had had to protect myself in some field, to fight for survival in my own way – to fight for some evolving soul, some evolving part.

Part of me has never felt more religious, and the purpose of this whole planet is almost hallowed to me. It is like you sense the purpose of everything. But I don't know what that purpose is and I am quite happy with that, whereas the enquiring engineer years ago would have wanted to know. Now I know I can't, so there is no longer any problem. I now see myself with a deep, deep appreciation of God but not in a definable, theological sense, only in existence itself. God doesn't need a definition for me any more. Anything I define it as just brings it down, in terms of the experiential relationship I'm talking about, into something that is a pale reflection and limitation of what it really is. Before God was simply conceptual, and at that period the truth that existed in my life was based on a conceptual relationship with life. I think I am now beginning to realise if a truth exists it is experiential; it is not conceptual, it doesn't have a defined limit of my mind.

Devo *As you were moving away from the psychic phenomena you were becoming increasingly more objective about life.*

Yes, and the function of meditation was becoming much greater. At first long periods of my life up here at Peacefields, where I now live, were spent in deep meditation. The effect of that was to highlight all the conceptual limitations and values that I had of life. Deep within our own psychological makeup, within I guess our own subconscious, lie the foundations of our own psychological behaviour. I think if you set about a process of deep inner investigation you almost bring an observable reality to those deep experiences.

Let me give you an example that occurred to me here, which at the time I gave incredible importance to but which now I really place no value on. In deep meditation one day the candles in my meditation room appeared to spontaneously ignite and I observed a remarkable vision above them. I doubted my own sanity and the validity of this experience. The candles then also spontaneously extinguished. After the experience I placed my finger into the candles and found that the wax was indeed hot. The effect of that was amazing because whereas I could accept that psychic phenomena could exist within the brain, almost like it was a separate psychological thing, I could not come to terms with a physical manifestation of that nature. I couldn't, it just blew me completely.

I put an enormous credence onto that experience at the time. It took one of the students that I was working with at a retreat in Sennen to bring me abruptly to a standstill with this. When I started to talk about this experience this beautiful lady turned to me at the end and said, "So what!" The effect of that was electric because I began to realise how I was winding myself up into another further limitation of my mystical journey, and that I was attempting to make a truth, a belief system.

The phenomena of the experience that happened during my meditation do not need explaining, it was simply a movement within the experience of life itself. Any explanation of it is a diversion, a branch of the tree, and if you climb along that branch it will snap. You must carry on climbing the main trunk, you must ignore the temptations of your own psychology to limit your own survival within some truth. You have got to break out of that.

DEVO *What do you mean by sitting in deep meditation?*

First of all I would structure the day in a physical way. I would start at four o'clock in the morning and sit for an hour or two. Similarly I would spend an hour or two every day in the afternoon as well, and in the evening I would perhaps spend another hour. So there were several hours a day of deep sitting. What I mean by deep sitting is the slowing of the whole process of my mental movement down to something that is almost tangible, that doesn't really seem to express much difference to life as it appears. It is almost like a breath on the surface of water. There is stillness there, no roughness. There is no impediment to the natural movement of life as it is. I would use my breath, or the movement of my abdomen breathing in and out, that is the nearest life source we have in terms of our own existence, and I would take it very, very deeply and very, very quietly, almost as if it were an end in itself. There is no diversion outside of that, and if a diversion occurs it simply passes, it doesn't have a credibility that can bring about an interruption of that movement of breath.

It is very hard to explain to a student what this really means at such a level of work because it takes years of practice to achieve, but the diversionary nature of one's own ambition of meditating or ego, if you like, is almost non-existent. The very breath has a value in itself that is complete; you don't have to stand outside of it.

It is as if the whole experience of the universe rests with my breath, and that is the beginning and end of it. If thoughts do emerge, they emerge in a very infrequent way and they simply pass. They are not able to pick up anything from the importance of the experience of the breath. And what eventually comes out of this is a deep realisation that you are your breath, there is nothing else. This creates an incredible contradiction because all of your mental strength is summoned towards demanding an existence of survival that is beyond that simple place. But in reality that is all you are, you are simply the breath.

DEVO *What do you mean by calling this period of time a mystic phase?*

I mean that the relationship to life was actually starting to change in its dimensional perspective, time was almost seen as a linear concept. It is not simply expansive or diminutive. At that point there is a wholly different relationship, and everything that comes out of that experience is me. And that is all "I" am. There is no place of separation, there is no movement of separateness outside of that other than what I make of it, which is my mental process. It is almost like the brain has a capability of being absolutely open to everything with no demand of anything. Any demand that is made of anything is me, it is I, it is who "I" am. I am the process of making something of that everything. That becomes a substantial experience to the mystic. What it does is it turns the whole relationship upside down, and the way you approach a situation is almost as if it is coming from the opposite direction.

An incredible trauma arose as a consequence of doing this work. I was finding myself inevitably drawn into my own koan. On the one hand was my own demand of life, for example that I should be a wise man, a guru perhaps, and on the other the realisation that there was no one to demand it. The two things together were epitomised for me in the metaphor of hanging onto a cliff and being afraid to let go. This went on, as far as I can remember, for six weeks of deep trauma. And when I did let go nothing happened, but everything changed.

I have read other people's account that it is a sort of one off transformational thing. For me that was not so; something physically has changed in the brain and that is a permanent thing.

In Vipassana at the very start of the teaching one of the main things one is told is that there is no thinker, simply the process of thinking. The full understanding of what this means is never realised until the end. In itself Vipassana is a limitation; it involves the total practice of the monk, an understanding of Buddhism, a whole belief system – the eightfold path, the four noble truths. And the realisation that there is no thinker comes out of an experience of a totally different relationship than that within Vipassana itself. It doesn't make sense I know. That is why I find myself being more and more zen, because in a way I find that is the only way I can move, "I" being the interpretation I am placing on the experience. That experience doesn't have a defined limit; it is only limited by me, "I", the process of thinking. So you realise as an experience that there isn't a thinker, there is simply the process of thinking. In the early stages that comes as an immense shock in its challenge, because you face yourself. You face yourself in your own survival. It is like a force of survival that you are facing head on, and the consequences of it are very dire in terms of your own identity and your own existence.

Devo *What was this letting go after weeks of deep trauma?*

There is an experience which we now call kensho, having cribbed the term from Zen, an experience where you become free of the need to maintain an identity in the experience of life itself. That doesn't mean that you have changed. This is the ridiculousness of it. It simply means that you carry on as you are but everything is free. It's nonsense I know.

Devo *So when the woman at Sennen said, "So what", that suddenly bought you up about the psychic experiences?*

I think she made me realise that there wasn't any validity in me pursuing my own ego into this psychic place, which is what I was doing. In other words, look what a clever bloke I am, look what I've achieved, what a great meditator I am, how spiritual. All that to me is simply an attempt to portray some enlightened stage that you feel you have reached. And it doesn't have any value.

Devo *And as a result of that did you stop meditating?*

No, the reverse was the case. I actually increased my meditating because I began to realise that there was a whole new relationship to be found which I had only just touched on up until then. That was the freedom from needing to make something of the experience of life. It didn't mean I would wake up in the morning and not go and buy something to eat or not go and try and make some money to live. That had nothing to do with it.

Devo *So although you were still meditating in a way you had lost any desire of meditation, any ambition of it, any goal of it.*

I think that is true; for me it was the final twist. I began to realise that sitting doing meditation up until that point had been for a purpose. I then realised the value of sitting in itself. It has a value in itself and does not require a purpose. The value of the experience lies in the breath itself. It doesn't have a value outside of that.

Devo *How did what you now call kensho come about?*

That came about with Rosemary. She had been working with me for six or so years, working very steadfastly with me and there was no student I had at that time who worked so intensely. Finally she went through an incredibly traumatic experience as well and came out in a different place. But she had no relationship to the psychic phenomena that I had experienced. At first I couldn't understand what was going on, but when I spoke with her I began to realise she had had a very profound experience, very akin to my own. The more I spoke with her the more I realised it was the same experience, and that therefore there must be many different journeys to that place. It was at this time when looking through a Zen book I came across a definition of the word kensho. I asked her whether she was experiencing a state in which no separate self exists. She said absolutely. I realised at that moment that that was exactly what I had experienced too, but I had not been able to separate it from all the external relationships of psychic phenomena, pathways, ladders that had led me to that place. I saw that there was a place there that I had arrived at like she had, but that she had done so from an entirely different direction. I realised that if this were true then each individual would approach it in a different way.

This realization of no separation, of no separate self, of no "I", no me, would appear to only happen through some incredible trauma, or experience of confrontation. But what I have now learned from the experience with half a dozen people here going through this is that there are many different ways the trauma can happen. Often it comes about through the interaction with others rather than through the interaction with just yourself. It isn't something you can control. It is something that is brought about, it seems to me, in an experiential way. You sow the seed by asking yourself who you are and you follow that through to a degree which is not simply conceptual but is an experiential movement within your own brain. For me the question "Who am I?" arises from a place of deep meditation, it is an experience not a concept.

At first this question "Who am I?" did not form the mainstay of my work in the way that it now does. I feel that the way I now teach and work with people is much more direct than my own experience was. I think as you cut away all the crap you begin to see the simplicity of the thing, and you begin to see how complex you have made it with all your ideas around it. You begin to shed them all, you don't need them. You can reduce it down to a great simplicity. And at the same time the more simple it becomes the more profound it becomes.

But what I do find is that it takes a long time for the student to realise that the value of all their belief systems has only been in their own need of them. Soul, higher self, karma, reincarnation, chakras or whatever provided them with a security for the self. It is all part of a growth basis from which their own self-survival works and if they have the courage, and it takes considerable courage, the question of "Who is I?" bypasses these limitations. The experience of seeing it in that way is then so much bigger, so much freer. It is a quantum leap.

DEVO *Would you say your work here for several years now is more like confronting people, finding ways of pointing people to that self-confrontation?*

I am not too sure about this because my views of it are constantly changing with my experience. When a person arrives here you start to chip away by saying, for example, well you are a Christian, why do you have Christian views? What you are immediately doing by asking that question is asking them to confront not just their Christian beliefs but their need to have any religious understanding. And when they confront that they begin to realise that having such beliefs are important parts of their identity to maintain their own validity and survival within life. As you chip away at these beliefs you begin to see their insecurity mount to a point of intense challenge, and they begin to realise that they are incredibly vulnerable.

DEVO *And that insecurity can be hopelessness, anger, despair.*

Anything arising at that moment out of our work. Even trying to rubbish our work is an attempt to create another identity. But we are not placing a concept in its place, we are challenging the reason why they need any concept. The effect of simply realizing that they need their concepts because they need to survive is to throw them back on themselves. I think that is the seed of kensho, is what creates that experience. It isn't something I do. It is something they do to themselves. I am a sort of reflective agent in that.

DEVO *When you are talking about security, survival you are talking of the sense of ego, the identity we have built up over our lives, who we think we are, who we think we must be in order to be able to continue living.*

In the ultimate sense you realise you are your ego, there isn't anyone to be egotistical with. The survival mechanism, which has the three attributes of identity, possessiveness and ambition, is essentially who you are. It is a genetic need to survive within the brain and it manifests itself in terms of creating the illusion of "I" or me as a separation, as a separate person, the illusion that somewhere in this body a David really exists. The only problem is you can't find a separate self, a me, "I", and when you cannot find such a self you find yourself to be challenged by the need to have a separateness. That is the whole basis of our work here.

DEVO *Going back to the experience of kensho, although at the time you didn't know that term, kensho was really when metaphorically you let go of the cliff after those six weeks.*

It was the realisation that there wasn't a separate self, because when I did let go I realised "I" didn't exist. And that is why nothing changed, because there was nothing to change other than freedom from the demand of self up to that point that I did exist. Now that doesn't mean that I have become fatalistic and lost the will to survive, it doesn't mean anything of the sort. In fact in some ways I feel I have a greater will to live because I have seen the perfection of the process itself. But the fear at the time was that I wouldn't carry on existing, that I would disappear in some way.

DEVO *That you would die?*

At least mentally if nothing else.

DEVO *When did that realisation of no separate self happen?*

There were four occasions. The first occasion was back at the Andrea Court Centre I was living and teaching in before I came here, when one morning I had the most incredible experience of there not being a separate self. But it went.

The second experience, again at Andrea Court, was when three of us were meditating in the main hall. I felt almost as if I was going into a trance, for this was post-medium days. But I knew it was different, there wasn't the same pull there, there wasn't quite the same feeling about it, my reactions weren't the same. I became aware I could see the front of the building, I could see the person who was on office duty that day, I could see her walking around. And then the telephone started to ring and when she picked it up there wasn't anyone there, and the telephone rang in the office and it also rang on the extension, something it didn't normally do without it being put through. I found myself talking as if I was answering the questions which Lyn, who was one of those sitting with me, was asking. But Lyn wasn't actually speaking the words out loud. The other person there said she felt very calm and very peaceful. I became so incredibly hot I started to sweat from head to foot, which wasn't unusual in a trance state but was very unusual in the state in which

I was now finding myself. The process went on for maybe an hour or so. At the conclusion of it a favourite leather belt of mine which I used to wear all the time had gone completely sticky, tacky and had stuck to my trousers, quite an incredible thing, and we had to throw it away afterwards. I had never seen leather change its texture like that, it seemed almost impossible that the body could get that hot, especially through material.

By describing things that were happening which other people also experienced I am trying to give an account verifiable by those outside of me. For at the time outside verification seemed to me quite important in order to show that it wasn't just my own imagination.

I was certainly different after that experience, as I have been with other experiences I have had. I think the important thing was the difference in the way I approached a situation rather than in some sort of vision or psychic power. It is like the organization of my mind was changing, there was an internal reorganization going on. I was starting to approach things in a completely different way after that day, and it seems to me when I look back on it, though at the time I may not even have been aware of it, it was setting about a different method in my mind. I do not really believe there was some external force in that, albeit at the time I think I felt there might have been some such force involved, a contact with something outside in the universe. The phenomena that surrounded it I'm not able to explain and I would guess anyone reading this would be very sceptical, because it is only my relationship to it.

I believe in hindsight that its importance for me was in the way it changed my attitude to life, in the way that I saw, for want of a better word, my spiritual work at that time and the way that I worked with it. I became much more self sufficient as a consequence of those experiences, less dependent on any ideological interpretations, much more self-aware that I am my own master. I think that is what came out of all this. Up until those series of experiences, like anyone else, I had a whole ideological dependency, whether Buddhist or any other, on some relationship with the universe.

DEVO *If you wanted to put an ideological interpretation on this, you could put one in terms of Hinduism and chakras and kundalini energy. That was never part of your belief system?*

No, and because it wasn't part of my belief system I wouldn't have put the same identity on it. This is the important point I think because I had not grown up with any Hindu connection at all and therefore Hinduism wasn't part of my beliefs. I think if it had been then I could well have decided that I had reached a particular place, some level. I think that would have been a disaster for me because if someone says to you such and such an effect means you have reached a special place then you become content in the belief that that is what it is. What I have grown to realise in my work here is that there is no such thing as a place and there is no such thing as an end; it is an unending quest of self-evolvement and self-development. There isn't a nirvana to reach.

I think realizing that is the big one, and allows a freedom which is greater than any limitation of it. Setting a limit of kundalini or any limit on an experience is a diminution of the reality of the experience. In reality there is no limitation other than what you make of it. I think that is very important. We have much more authority in terms of our experience than we give ourselves credit for. Much more authority, because that is who we are, we are the experiencing energy, we are the experiencing force.

The third one was the candle experience out here, which I have already talked about, and post that was the realisation of the cliff itself. I had known the cliff was there because I had sensed it before; this is a metaphor you understand, it is not a physical cliff! And even back in the pre-Andrea Court days I had felt that there was this void, this black void of fear, of uncertainty. It would heighten itself at times, it would come at me at times, and I guess at those moments I would run from it.

DEVO *Void is a good word, and that void was that if you let go, if you didn't hold yourself back, you would disappear into that void and that would somehow be the end of you?*

Yes, almost like a black hole.

Devo *So in a way you backed off it. But finally on the fourth time ...*

Something permanently changed. I think what happened is it culminated in me not being prepared to retreat any more, and then at that point there was no way back. I changed. There is no cliff, there is no one to hang on, there is no void even. These were all manifestations of my own fear for survival.

Devo *This experience happened when you were meditating?*

It went on for six weeks in the end. I wasn't sitting for six weeks, it was a thing that was constantly working with me. When I talked with Rosemary it was a thing that went on with her for a period of time – there were moments when she would find herself running in sheer terror. That was how it manifested for her. There is a moment when it happens and that is almost like an instant, everything is different from that moment on. It is like you wake up from a dream, suddenly you wake up, you have had this terrible dream. There is a freedom there, and suddenly the hole in your heart has gone. You don't wake up and say, "Wow, the hole in my heart has gone, I'm free." The perspective has changed, and everything you view looks different, but at the same time is the same. The tree looks exactly the same but there is a different dimension to it than there was before.

Devo *But also internally you look exactly the same, your ego is exactly the same, but there is a whole different perspective.*

Yes, you almost appreciate your ego. Ego is the perfection of how you survive. So you find yourself behaving in an identical way as before, yet everything has changed. The perspective has changed and it is almost like you are coming from the opposite way.

I realise now that kensho is just the start. You then have a lifetime's work because it is like you are chasing yourself through your own ideological limitations of the brain, you are going into every corner of your life. I'm fifty-eight years old and there is an awful lot of accumulated material up there, many experiences and often they don't show themselves, but then something happens and one does show itself. And then you see the anomaly. It is like you have this ability to see an anomaly. You have an ability to instantly pick up the separations you are making even as you start to make them. You can see the others here who have experienced kensho also have that ability to catch the separation in themselves and in others too. It is like it's just there, it's so blatant, it's so simple. It feels so obvious that why can't others see it? Well of course the reason the other person can't see it is because they believe they are separate from what they are saying and doing. Whereas through kensho you can see that is who they are. It is like a different place, it is so obvious.

Mindfulness, being aware and catching the separation, is almost like breathing to me now. It is as if it has become second nature, part of my make up. It is not something that I have to be conscious of constantly, not something I am doing, having to remember. If you look at the martial arts, to give an example, you can see someone who has gone through the various grades to achieve an optimum in a particular art. People will come at him or her in various ways and the martial artist's reflexes happen almost unconsciously, it has become their second nature. In a similar way if you have mastered the art of mindfulness it has just become part of you. So if I were to ask myself, "Who am I?" the answer would be, I am the process of being mindful. That is who "I" am, I don't exist beyond that.

> DEVO *Is it still from the need to survive that you are immediately able to see the way in which you are creating a separate identity of self?*

The difference is, I think, that I am conscious of what I am doing, and that that is who "I" am and I can't be anything other than that. Whereas people who haven't experienced kensho are not conscious of this. They believe they are something separate doing whatever it is they are doing. There is a difference, there really is a difference. Now the effect for the person who is in the space of kensho is it produces an immense freedom because you don't have to be anything other than what you are. What you are is all there is.

The work I'm doing now with the group has moved on far beyond even that. We are moving into areas of beginning to understand a universal relationship to the experience of kensho. This is something much greater and is something I didn't even dream of in the early days.

Devo *What do you mean by universal relationship?*

That what I am is all there is, and if an objective reality exists outside of that I do not know that. This is a whole new sphere of understanding. It is not based on conceptual conjecture, it is based on the experience that I create my own reality. As you chip away at this it becomes clearer and clearer and clearer. Now I am not the first one to say this, individual mystics have said it for thousands of years.

Devo *So in working with the various students in the group your own understanding is deepening.*

Much, much more. It is being accelerated because it needs to be accelerated in order to keep up with their development. There is a learning of the extensiveness of it. What happens as you evolve in the process is like a drop of dye in a bowl of water, its colour spreads and spreads into every action of the day. And you begin to realise that relationship is also true with others and is true in their relationship with you.

It becomes a very interactive thing, so it is almost like someone standing there and saying, there is this and there is this too. And they are opening their hands to a new experience that is part of it as well, one that in some ways you almost hadn't acknowledged to be part of you. It is an experience that can cover everything you can possibly think of, there really is no exception. So it seems that in the interaction that is created as I have a discourse I am learning a great deal. If I didn't talk to someone I couldn't get that learning experience to the breadth and extensiveness that I do.

It must be changing me because I am a constant evolving process, I am not something with a fixed limit. There is a freedom once you acknowledge that; because you are an evolving process you are not the same person today as you were. You don't have to be what you were yesterday, you have a right to go forward. You have the right to change your mind in the experience of life and not narrow it down to some datum from the past. That is a tremendous freedom, but that freedom can only occur if you are not trying to defend a self and maintain a security of a self.

To me where religions often go wrong is that they set an absolute and then everyone has to conform to that absolute regardless of their experience of what is happening around them. It's almost like religion holds everything in a straitjacket of belief systems that it is unable to break out of.

There is a most beautiful saying, "The ways to the One are as many as the lives of men." I don't think there is a correct way to approach this work of ours. What is important is to stimulate the investigative nature of the seeker to the point where they can set off on their own exploration, then they can expand to their own experience. There isn't one belief system that is right and one that is wrong. To me life is belief systems, a whole agglomeration of them. Ideas and different places, that is life really; that is who we are, we are our belief systems. It is quite beautiful.

The Taoist Stallholder

When I was working on the markets, there was a cockney guy there with a great big stall next to mine. We probably had two of the biggest stalls on the market. It used to take us ages to set them up, and he was a crafty sod because he used to keep on taking more and more ground. What you do on a market is you pay for so much a foot of frontage, and he would wait until the toby, that's the guy who collects the money, had gone past and then he would start spreading his stall out. I wouldn't let him spread it my way, I'd kick up hell about it, but he'd spread it out in other directions. He was constantly in trouble with the market authority because he was always doing something wrong. I also used to get very agitated with that particular market authority because they were very dictatorial and I used to get really uptight. But what he did was he waited until the toby had gone and he moved his stall out a foot. The guy would come back and say, "look you've moved it out again." "Oh God, I'm sorry, yes," and he'd put it back again. The toby would go away and he'd put it out again. He never got upset about it, he just kept taking as much as he wanted and in the end the authority gave up. He used to do what the hell he liked because every time he said, "I'm very sorry," and then he'd put it out again. I couldn't do that because there was a principle at stake, my right and the authority's right, my desire of how they should behave. So I wouldn't break the rules because I was standing by what was fair and right whereas he didn't give a sod. He wore them down. It's like a sponge, you can hit it and it gives way, and when you pull your fist out it comes back out again. They couldn't win. They wrote him letters, they did all sorts of things. Clever, clever understanding about the demand of life, very Taoist. I learnt a lot from that guy.

That market trader had decided what he was going to do. He understood his conditioning, he worked with the experience, and when the experience confronted him he retreated and when it retreated he came forward, and that was it. A real Tai Chi at work.

Meditation

You are your thinking process, but you can't think two thoughts at once. So what happens as a string of thoughts comes through is that although there may be a nanosecond difference only one thought is possible at a time. Normally your mind is turning over at such a rate that it becomes very difficult to see each thought separately. That speed creates the illusion of a separate self. We need to slow that flow down, we need to make the nanosecond almost a second, or two or three just to space it out so we can see the thought process in itself. Then the whole process becomes very apparent.

Vipassana meditation slows the thinking process down to a point where we can be aware of a thought arising in our minds. In one of his essays D.T.Suzuki says the same, that the real merit of vipassana is in the slowing down of the thinking process. Other forms of meditation set about achieving an objective. In Christianity we have contemplative prayer, which is a form of meditation, in Hinduism various types of devotional meditations, in Buddhism over sixty types of meditation each one designed for a specific purpose. But if we take away the Buddhist ideology surrounding it, vipassana is essentially a tool of self-reflection through focusing on the breath. Other contemporary Buddhist teachers have done the same. We have tried here to not even be Buddhist about it. We are simply being methodical about it.

In the busy environment of everyday life, things come and go so fast that it becomes very difficult to see where you are in relation to your work in terms of self-realisation. But when you slow down the thinking process through the practice of meditation you can clearly see what is arising and falling away. The tool of vipassana allows all the desires to be understood, how they come in, how you constantly try and make something of them.

To give an illustration of the relationship such a slowing down has to our work here, let's just imagine that the carpet on the floor represents our existence. I put my glasses case on the carpet to represent the mind. Now let us limit the way this case can move to just the two horizontal dimensions, back and forth across the carpet, and exclude the third, vertical dimension. Obviously there are really three dimensions, but I am making it two-dimensional so I can draw what I call the extra dimension in relationship to it. So now I am a two-dimensional man who believes that all of my existence is dependent on me moving solely in either of two ways. This glasses case travelling across the carpet is my life, my reality, my universe. At no time, because of my two-dimensional limitation, do I relate to the third dimension.

It is the same when we practise meditation. Any desires we have of meditation are on this two-dimensional plane. Many Buddhists who practice vipassana see this slowing down process as an advantage, because if my mind isn't tearing everywhere it is going to be more restful, more harmonious. But these are simply fringe benefits, therapeutic benefits, which don't have a relationship to what we are talking about here. The experience of mysticism however isn't dependent on you moving in either of the two directions. Your identity, existence and survival are dependent on that. The problem is that you define mysticism as having a value only if it can have a value to your existence, to your desire. It cannot have a value any other way.

As I slow down the process of charging in different directions I start to become aware that the desire I place in the movement of myself is itself the separating force. By slowing down I can just stand still and become awake to my reality. Instead of going blindly into the direction of my desire, I just stand in the awareness of the moment, what in Buddhism is called objectively, allowing the whole experience to come to me. What I start to realise then is that there is something else taking place. In the quietude of such a moment there is a totally different experience, one that cannot be compared to everyday life, cannot be compared to survival, because it consists of a vertical awareness into another dimension. The mind cannot assimilate it nor make any sense of it because the mind, in our analogy, can only function two dimensionally and this experience is three-dimensional.

You ask me what value is this new dimension to the mind and I say none, only all value because in that experience the carpet is seen at a glance. It is not seen in a specific direction, it is seen in its totality and then no part of the carpet is seen as having a greater or lesser value. To rise above the carpet does not have any value to me because I cannot use it. I can only use the carpet when I move along it, and moving along it is a two-dimensional journey not a three-dimensional observation. This third, vertical dimension can have no value to the two-dimensional movement because it is not about either of the two directions, it is about everything. So no amount of preparation or simile or metaphor can create an understanding of what that experience is. The experience is a total vision of life, it is not something we make of life. Mysticism, in our illustration, is not a two-dimensional relationship but a three-dimensional one.

The desire that is motivating me across this carpet has no relationship to the experience that occurs in mysticism. In fact it is a limitation of the mystical experience. But you have got to survive you say, you have got to walk on the carpet of life, you cannot just stand in one place, you have got to go to work everyday, you have got to exist in the real world. Yes you have, but if you are awake to that reality at each moment the mystical reality always exists; it never does not exist.

Somehow by the nature of kensho the mind no longer has a desire of finding anything one way or another in relation to the movement of trying to make sense of life. The mind has given up all such desire because what motivates it is the perfection of its own survival; not an attempt to resolve that survival. In kensho the perfection is seen and accepted simply as it is within its own movement.

IVOR *If I am careful when meditating to keep my attention on the changes at either end of the breath then I find I can almost be without any thoughts. It's not that I don't have them but I am simply aware that they are floating around somewhere below the level of my attention.*

So you have got to the point where the breath is the breath and thoughts just fall away, but behind that there is still a secret desire for something else to happen. The glasses case in this analogy is still moving across the carpet. At the moment when there is no desire, the breath is as it is. Then the experience is as it is. When there is no movement away then suddenly there is a realisation of something else. Now, immediately that happens you try and make something else of it, and you again start moving the glasses case across the carpet. As the mind reacts, what I call the "wow" factor comes in. Let it go, what's the big deal? Why "wow" it, why do that? Only because you are trying to find something there for you, and I am telling you there is nothing. The experience isn't about giving yourself something.

The problem is how do you tell a two-dimensional being that there exists a third dimension that he can experience? What you have to do, is say it isn't any way that I move the glasses case across the carpet. It is as it is, don't try and make sense of it. What I am talking about isn't a method, it is an act of acknowledging my two-dimensional existence, acknowledging that I am doing nothing more than just moving the glasses case to and fro on the carpet.

The human mind is only designed to make sense, in our analogy, of the two-dimensional movement of the glasses case. But the act of doing that is a separation from the total experience. The experience is totally different, something mind cannot make sense of. You cannot think your way there. Totality exists as it does. "I" can't relate to that unless "I" make something of it. "I" am the process of making something out of totality, and that is a limitation of it. I can be more adept at it, I can have a much greater profoundness in the whole experience, but whatever I do will always be a limitation. The very ambitions that we set ourselves in the quietude of sitting are the ones that separate us.

What sometimes happens is that there is a momentary glimpse of the carpet as a totality. The circumstances are individual about how that happens from what I can see over many years of working with people. It can be an instant, an hour or two, several days, a week or more. These are often called peak experiences, which many of you have had.

MATTHEW *The other day for instance, after being here, when I was out in the street I had the experience of seeing myself in everybody. Whoever I looked at, young or old, man or woman, the flavour of who I think I am was reflected back to me regardless. The ability of the mind to register someone as different wasn't there. It was a very clear and extreme experience. We were all in the same soup.*

Let me suggest that you were seeing them as they are rather than as you wanted to see them. Ram Dass calls it falling in love with everybody. It is acknowledging my personal interpretation of each person.

LINDSEY *My peak experience was similar. One recent Sunday morning I was carving for a hundred or more people for two or three hours, and it was a continuous line of people. I was spending maybe thirty seconds with each person as they walked through. And then for a moment every single person that I looked at appeared beautiful – old and young. I had a huge rush of energy that went on for a few hours. It ended and afterwards I was tripping into a sense of knowingness – I knew things but didn't know how I knew them.*

I'd call that experience a satori. Now how should we deal with that experience? What limited it, and similar experiences of others here, to a few hours?

DEVO *It seems to me that if you move into this extra dimension the mind is caught unawares for a second and doesn't know what to make of it. Then the mind, because that is its habit, immediately comes back and kind of slips under the experience and starts sorting it out.*

Exactly, for when I am walking across this carpet in a two-dimensional plane, each moment that I come to is controlled by my desires of it, the directions I am taking, the uncertainties that I have. Then in some instant it is as if I see the whole carpet, I no longer see any specific relationship to the carpet, and that changes the way I act. There is that moment of experience that is held with me, in the instant.

I know the first time this happened to me, before kensho, was just like you have each described, and it was like that for days after. There was a different clarity about everything I did. It threw me totally.

Now the importance of that experience for me, and I am suggesting the importance for all of you, is it adds credibility to the experience of life. It shows me where it is, it becomes a substantial relationship. It is the litmus test of all these words that we throw around here. They are not what it is about, it lies with your own individual experience. Be aware of your individual experience for that is the datum from which you work.

The reason this clarity goes is because you define some desires. At the initial moment you understand, in our analogy, the totality of the carpet. The whole carpet is seen in a different way. Then the experience starts to go local again, it starts to get back into the moving of the glasses case around; more and more the impact of the experience is lost as if it is all funnelling back into a two-dimensional place again. You are trying to control it, even though you believe you are not, making it whatever you want it to be – awesome, light, bliss, love. You have a desire for it be perpetuated and to continue. And that is a limitation. What I am saying is that it is not simply a two-dimensional experience but two dimensions are the only way you can relate to it. As another student said to me once, you talk of opposites but at such a moment it is like I see both opposites simultaneously and in that sense the totality you talk of applies.

If you are like me, the first time it happens you are going to spend the next few days in meditation trying to work out some way to make it happen again. That is the worst thing you can do, because that is dialectically opposite to why you had the experience. The problem is that that is all the mind can do. At such a moment, because you aren't separate, you begin to see the beauty and the perfection of totality. But mind is about creating separation and identity.

Somehow we have to be aware that we are not going to resolve this by walking across the carpet. But we also have to acknowledge that that is what we have to do in order to survive. So the mystic carries on moving around the carpet like he or she has always done, but there isn't an ambition beyond that. At the moment of quietude, the breath is the breath; it is nothing neither more nor less than that. Then you can begin to glimpse the insight of J. Krishnamurti when he says: the more the tree is like the tree, the more it is like God. The more the breath is like the breath, the more it is the breath of God.

CHRISTO *Is that the same as saying it is difficult to be what is?*

The difficulty in being what is comes because you have got ideas of 'what is' is – enlightenment, self-realisation, awareness, consciousness, ordinariness, whatever you want to call it. Immediately you give up the idea of 'what is' is like, you start to experience what is. That is the difficulty. How can you resolve this? Here comes the paradox – **you** can't. What the koan does in Zen Buddhism is to look at that paradox and attempt to resolve what can't be resolved.

One Zen student I met in Austria had been given the famous koan, 'What is the Buddha nature of a dog?' He said that the answer is *Mu*, which literally translated means no. But it doesn't, it means nothing, and nothing not as a word but as nothing; it just doesn't have a translation. He said he had taken that koan and had worked with it, and it had freed him from the fear of death. I said, "So what? So now you are not afraid to die, but where does that take you?" Suddenly it was as if someone had switched a light on in his head. He understood that really all he was doing was participating in an advanced form of therapy, almost to suppress some desires that were arising.

What had happened, it seems to me, is that he had got caught in the procedure of koans, and indeed the Master who was leading him seemed to be caught in it as well. I think this is one of the dangers of believing a koan can be solved and so has a value. If you imply value you imply a purpose and if that purpose has even a hint of resolution, which it must do if I then give you a second koan, hasn't it failed? Only one koan should be needed, why another? Another is given because of the belief that there is a process leading to self-realisation, and this is something with which I strongly disagree. I think if the old Zen patriarchs were around now they wouldn't go along with that, because if there is a paradox to be addressed then the paradox has to be about giving up all demand of it. It is the only way it can be. It is not about just simply sitting back and trying to make your way through by following a procedure. You can't conceptualize this.

We use the whole process of paradox to defeat itself until in the end you give up – and then it can happen. The wisdom here is that the giving up is not a desire, but an action. It's an action of what I call freedom. It's experiencing the freedom of reality as it is, and that's not my or anyone's idea of freedom. It can never be my idea of freedom, because my idea of freedom is always limited to the horizontal plane of the carpet.

IVOR *I get a little confused with this giving up you are talking of, because I get to a certain point in meditation and I give up. Then I wonder whether I am giving up because I haven't tried hard enough or is this the right moment.*

Who is there to give up and who is giving up?

NISH *It is not a desire to give up. I know it personally. There is a desire to give up, either because you have heard you should or because you are fed up. Then you have a desire to give up, you don't just give up. You sit there and say: I give up, which is still a desire. So it is just another movement really.*

The reason it becomes so mammoth in your mind and so traumatic is because your whole survival is threatened. You can sit here forever saying, I give up, I give up, but at no time are you really challenging "me". That is just rhetoric giving "me" an idea about what giving up is. It is an experience and an action, it is not an idea. What actually gives up in the end is the very desire itself to give up, the desire to achieve enlightenment, liberation, or whatever you want to call it. **You** can't do it because you are the desire, and you can't separate yourself off from that desire by another desire because that further desire is also you. You can't make it happen, because you would then be the person making it happen. You would have created another force of separation.

NISH *In "Zen in the Art of Archery" the author, Herrigel, gets taught by a Master archer. He is shooting for months. He is told it's about letting go and he is told that the fingers have to let go on their own. Then he finds a way to make them let go without purpose. He was really proud and he said I've got it, I've got it, showing it to his Master. The Master was very quiet and said, show me again, so he showed him again. The Master turned around, walked out the hall and walked away. He wouldn't come back because Herrigel had come up with a deception, and that archery Master saw it as a deception. It took Herrigel weeks and weeks of begging to be taught again. This is a good example I think of how the mind comes up with a solution. It will always come up with a solution.*

In archery the arrow is there and that is the beginning and end of it, the zen of it. It is the thinking mind that works out how the arrow gets there and thereby separates itself. The arrow is there; it never was not there.

You can't have it, and once you understand that, you can begin to see the process of separation you are making. The koan that drives you to distraction is the need, in the carpet analogy, to resolve it two dimensionally. You can't do it; what you desire is 'desire less'. But acknowledging what it isn't opens the doors to what it is. It's not something you can have, and it takes quite incredible courage to let that desire go, because you desperately need an identity in it. Kensho is simply an ability, though it's not really ability, more a knack, not to demand an identity from everything as an experience.

CHRISTO *Is there actually a part that is not part of the "I", an individual consciousness?*

If there is a totality there must be an energy of totality, and if that's what you mean by consciousness the answer is yes. But it is not you, it is not individual. I call it the "plurality of consciousness". That "plurality of consciousness" is not an individual thing, though you desperately want it to be. Yet you are it as well, because you are how it recognizes that it exists. So I say the "plurality of consciousness" isn't you nor me, it is us; but you or me is how we know it exists.

CHRISTO *If there is no thinker just a thought process what is it in vipassana that recognizes this thought process?*

Another thought. This may still be having thoughts about thoughts, observer and observed. It is what J. Krishnamurti calls standing in a different corner of the same field. You are putting another screen in front called awareness. He is absolutely right, but the point I am making is we have to do that in order to slow the process down.

CHRISTO *What is this awareness?*

It is the thinking process, but it is a thinking process that is seeking to understand its identity with that process itself. It is moving in a slightly different way, reflecting it. So I acknowledge that if I am aware of something, I have created another thought about another thought.

As thoughts arise at each moment in time, we have to be aware not only of the thought arising but of our conditioned environment, for this creates the limitation we expect that thought to operate within. Otherwise if we are not careful we end up with further restrictions and limitations. If we are aware of this possibility then we don't have to be the victim of it. Unless you can be open to how your conditioning shapes your expectations you will create a limited approach to this work. And you will do this in such a way that you will never be able to break through the limitation that you set on it in terms of your experience. This is how self defends itself within experience.

LYN *If we are doing some meditative practice, say vipassana at certain times in the day, how is self going to hide in that?*

In the practice itself. In order to do it properly for example, I may believe that first of all I have to light an incense stick and a candle, that I have to find an appropriate cushion, that I have to sit in a lotus or a half-lotus position and have my hands in the mudra of meditation, the thumbs not touching. If I don't get it right then I have have no identity as a meditator because I'm not doing it properly. Whereas it shouldn't matter a damn. I could just as well sit in a cosy armchair with my legs crossed and a pillow under my head. The point is not that the practice of meditating is wrong. It is the expectation of what the practice is, the desire you have of it, that is wrong because then you are trying to get to a place of identity and survival for your "self". This is simply perpetuating the separation from the actual experience. So I used to shave my head, wear robes and live like a monk in order to achieve what I thought was liberation. This was doing just the same thing, and it is not about that at all. Unless you understand this you can be caught, and it will catch you in every moment. Self will hide in the practice itself, and then the method is not seen simply as a method but as the identity that is needed.

Your environment can be a clue, for the mind might conceive that it can only happen where it has happened before, whereas in reality it can happen anywhere. In fact it usually happens where you are not expecting it because then you have no expectation of that place. For example, one of the students here was at the end of a ski slope and he just took off. The adrenalin was flying and he was totally mindful, he dared not be anything else because his life was on the line. And it happened. But then the next time he did the same thing it didn't happen, because his expectation of the environment had become limited to it happening by jumping down the ski slope.

Someone else was with me and I held up a glass and on one occasion she had an incredible experience and on the next occasion nothing, because then she was looking for something. She had limited the environment down to that, her meditation had become me holding a glass. It doesn't matter where you do it, how you do it or what you do; it is simply being able to get yourself to self-reflect what is happening in your mind.

The mystical experience is always available wherever and however you are. It is just that you simply aren't open to it, you are not awake to it. We are too busy shooting off in one direction or another, and even at the point of standing still every expectation and desire we have in doing that creates a limitation. So I go to the meditation room to meditate. Why? There is no reason, just do it because it's there.

NISH *On the way here this morning I was thinking we have said that we are how God knows itself. So the first thing me hearing that would be yes, there is a God and he knows himself through me. I make separations all the way, between God, me and something that is seen or experienced. So I am a whole chain of separations. And that of course is completely opposite to what is actually said. That statement can only make sense if you stop making these separations and start to see it can't happen with the separations. So God, me and the seen cannot be separate.*

I don't know if you can get the zen of this, but equally it can't happen without them. You see, and we are going to be very simplistic here, going back to the carpet analogy a moment, "the plurality of consciousness" is looking at the carpet as a whole from the vertical standpoint. But this consciousness can only know itself through me and you moving across the carpet. Unless you are two dimensionally placed within that three-dimensional experience it couldn't do that. In the same way the illusion of separation is necessary for the tree outside, for example, to recognize itself through you the moment you look at it. Mysticism is about the collapse of that illusion.

DEVO *In Advaita they talk about the True Self, that rather than an individual self there is something universal, often called consciousness, which is all there is. You sometimes talk about everything. Does that everything in any way correspond?*

I believe that if you talk about universal energy, universal love, God, consciousness, you could describe a thousand different things, all you have done is broken it into small pieces and called it one of those things. Everything to me is an encompassment of totality. It doesn't have a separation; you are the process of making it separate. Apart from that there is no reality. Now what you are suggesting is that there is a reality external to the separateness that I make of life. Well if there is, how do "I" know that, because "I" am the product of making something separate.

In Vipassana, consciousness and awareness are simply expressions of the opposites. Consciousness is a subjective process, consciousness is the process that says and names – there's the bench, there's the tree. Consciousness is the conscious action of the mind, seeking and moving constantly with its desires. Awareness is an objective state, not a subjective one. It stands back and it allows the image to come to me without defining it as a seat, as a tree. So awareness is the objective openness, consciousness is the subjective process. They are just definitions, but understanding this you can then begin to make sense of the Buddha's difference between looking and seeing, listening and hearing. Consciousness looks, consciousness listens; awareness sees, awareness hears. The Buddha says, if I see and if I hear, I am awake.

If we create a conscious force, we automatically create an aware force, and if we create an awareness or objective view we immediately create a subjective view. We can't help doing that. Being awake in the truest sense is neither of these but both. It is the experience of being able to see both sides simultaneously. When I have got nothing to gain from this, when I have made no preference of this, then everything is, and I simply react to everything.

Now every time Ivor sits he is looking for a preference. He says that is not true because when he is sitting he is dealing solely with his thoughts, they are just simply arising and falling away. But in the background is a preference that meditating should lead to something. He is still defining the horizontal movement of the glasses case across the carpet as being a solution. He is not allowing the glasses case to rise above the carpet, a happening which is of itself, not of any demand. It is a reaction of mind with no identity. So in that moment there is no need of it, there is no desire of it, it is as it is. That is awesome if you like, awesome because I have suddenly realised the perfection of it all, I no longer have a desire of it. But what happens is the human mind tries to make something of that – a blinding light, ordinariness, or even the tree being like a tree. Doing that is simply another restriction.

Ivor *When I stand still in my breath all sorts of movements happen outside my awareness.*

You have to find them, you have got to become aware of them. They are not outside your awareness, it is just you are not aware of them because you are them. The slowing down process allows you to see that.

Do you have a thought of your breath?

IVOR *I experience my breath going in and out.*

What is that, if it isn't a thought? Who is experiencing it? Go back to square one: Who is focusing on their breath?

IVOR *Ivor in some way.*

Well, who is that? It is a thought arising. There is no thinker, only a thinking process. Every mystic has said this. You are still maintaining you are a thinker. You still haven't grasped as an experience the concept that no thinker exists called Ivor, only a thinking process. I accept that at the moment it is only a concept for you. As long as you maintain that there is a thinker there is always a way out for you, the thinker. You have to understand that what is really being challenged is you the thinker. Who is Ivor? Is he a thinking process or does a thinker exist? As long as you can assure yourself that a thinker exists you are quite safe in observing your thoughts, and there isn't really a challenge.

Now don't believe you are going to get rid of the thinker just like that. It will be the biggest struggle that ever faced you in your life. All thoughts of fear, of insecurity that arise do so as a consequence of you being challenged about the thinker. Until you are prepared to face the possibility that no thinker exists you will always try and make sense and always try and have a thinker thinking, so a thinker can say there is a thought I am thinking. That is the trap you are in at this moment, you are not seeing that you are simply a thought.

Ask the question: Who is the thinker? Not by just repeating: Who am I? Who am I? For "Who am I?" is a question that goes to the very root of my movement itself. It is not one that just floats across the surface, because it is challenging who is asking that question. Take it as "Who is I?" if you want. "Who is I?" is the greatest koan that was ever created. Resolve it.

The totality I am talking about, the experience that I am hinting at, isn't a vacuum of nothing; it is everything. You could call it awesome but it is not something I can have, it is something I **am**. I am not offering you insecurity, but neither am I offering you security. I am offering you life as it is, and life as it is is your unique reaction to everything, not mine, not my ideas about it, not any of the analogies I've made.

The very first day I went and sat in a Buddhist meditation talk, I was told no such thing as a thinker exists. I understood that, but I didn't know what it meant. I didn't realise that it was the most profound statement I had ever heard, that it would present for me the greatest challenge of my life, and just that simple statement would take me into an experience that changed my life. It is true, it is so true.

Timelessness

The mystical experience has no value to you; all time is experienced simultaneously in four dimensions. But the four-dimensional experience is a total thing, it is everything; it is not something you can limit it back to, called self experiencing time in three dimensions.

Looking at the motive rather than any explanation, why should I need to define time? You do that in an attempt to identify a relationship with the totality. Timelessness exists as a relationship of no self, but self immediately tries to relate with that. In other words can I, David, be timeless? No, I, David, am the product of movement within my three-dimensional plane. My reaction will always happen dimensionally within the three planes. What you are hoping for is that you can carry that timelessness with you into your three-dimensional world, and you can't do that. So that timelessness is always with you but your consciousness of self as a separation can only define it in three dimensions.

Motivation

It has to be examined as to why you need to devote yourself to a faith, a belief system, an ideology or a person. You have to understand the motivation otherwise you behave blindly within your own conditioning.

Always look for the motivation. It is easy to understand in day-to-day activities, but something as profound as devotion has great depth within us. We need something to believe in, and we fear that to challenge our belief is to challenge our very existence. As you listen to a Guru the question needs to be asked, when you start to understand the process of motivation, what is the value to us of that Guru, Avatar or whatever? If we are able to understand our motivations we can understand the ideological separations we place on the experience of life itself. We then find that we don't actually need to challenge our ideological understandings. We can simply put them to one side and go back to the very core issue of survival that motivates us and so motivates our separation.

Working like this you begin to realise that motivations are not right or wrong, they are simply an attempt to create a self-identity in order to survive. We have the need to survive both as an individual and as a collective, as an intelligent ape and as a tribe. The power of our imagination turns the need to survive into many different ideas and beliefs. But the real clue is the motivating factor and that is always about survival – the need to find purpose in life, to find out who I am. If we can understand the motivations of our mind we can understand the restrictions and the limitations that we put on the experience of life itself. We can break the fetters, if you like, of our own limitation of experience. What actually leads beyond just the simple need to experience this room today? Why do we have to go beyond that point? Mysticism is about life as it is not what we think it is, for the thinking bit is our limitation.

ROSEMARY *You can only turn the question of motivation around when you start asking why you are asking the question, rather than looking for the answer. Because as long as you are looking for an answer you are not addressing where the question has arisen from, you never actually get beyond the answer, you just chase your tail.*

Like the tiger's tail in Buddhism you go round and round and round. So the key lies in finding the origin of the question not in finding an answer. But the nature of our mind is to seek an answer, and you head off into a place of concepts and beliefs. In seeking an answer is where mind again tricks itself.

To translate this into a reality in our lives we have to start with our relationship to life at this and every moment. We have to look at our reaction in terms of our mind to the experience that we are having. So however I am reacting, whether with sadness or with happiness, we have to ask the question why, rather than try to find a solution to our unhappiness or even to our happiness. The act of tracing back your motivations will take you through your own conditioning to that place of survival. When you reach survival, acknowledge it, there is no need to go any further. But it is no good doing this as an intellectual exercise. You have really got to go back through the levels to get to that point. You have to do it, no one can do it but you. And do it at that moment not afterwards, because by then you forget everything that has happened. What you will find is that there is a sequence and pattern of behaviour that is like a habit you get into.

The difficulty, as you look for what is motivating you, is that even in posing the question you are already caught up in the whole process. Because it is happening so fast, it is already too late by the time you have asked the question. What's happening is a whole sequence in which you are bound up. It is you after all, and you are caught in the endlessness of that. The beauty of vipassana meditation is in the slowing down of the mind process. When you are sat on the mat your whole mind becomes conscious of the process itself rather than of your ideas around it. And when you do slow down the thinking process you find that the self starts to disappear and you begin to see your motivations. You can then acknowledge the perfection of your motivation to survive and to create an identity within experience.

You will always have judgements of life because your survival is dependent on judgements. There isn't a harmony in the middle somewhere like many believe who teach meditation and say: "Just let it go." Who are you letting go? You can't let yourself go, that is you. It is not wrong, as many Buddhists argue, for me to have desires because desires are how I survive. Rather it is right to acknowledge them, to know and understand their relationship because joy is born of that. Joy is born within the contentment of experiencing life as it really is. If I am miserable it does not mean I ought not to be, that I ought to be happy, for there comes the judgement. It doesn't mean you have got to change your feelings, your mental attitudes. It is understanding what is happening, and that that is okay.

This is how within the perfection of it I see it differently, because I understand that my perfection is augmenting my desire to survive. It is simply acknowledging the way it is, acknowledging that your reaction is your perfection and that you are fine the way you are, because the way you are is motivated by your desire to survive.

Looking and understanding my motivations, I find, takes away their pressure. My judgement is simply understood and acknowledged. Happiness is not really related to whether the situation I am in satisfies my desires of it or not. Happiness is related to my relationship to life as it is. Happiness, joy, is a natural movement within myself about life as it really is; it is not something I can desire and generate.

Desire

Desire is the mind's alternative to what is. Desire is a conscious separation you create to interpret a unique relationship of being. So we make the experience good or bad, pleasurable or painful, and so on. Desire is wonderful, perfect, because no emotion is wasted, none at all, and so we create our own unique universe of movement, which is how nature experiences itself.

Consciousness, the subjective force of my mind projecting itself, is the tool of self-growth. Awareness, the objective force, standing back and seeing everything as it is, is the realisation. Desires, expectations, ideas and beliefs are a conscious interpretation of being by each of us uniquely, and we see them from the state of joy with compassion, almost as something external to us. We can see the perfection of them as our conscious reaction to the compassionate state of awareness. We can see and understand that these exclusive emotions we all feel are our unique relationship to being, are how consciousness knows itself. Desire is neither wrong nor right, it is just yours – your desire, your unique relationship, like mine is mine. It is the way it is, and it has within it a value that is unique to each of us, if we understand that. This is the value of knowing yourself. Suddenly everything drops away and you realise that what stopped you being was the separation you had placed on the desire, not the desire itself. Desire did not separate you, you had separated desire.

When I started my work I was told by my Teacher that you have to live in the present, just as an animal lives in the present. But by having a desire for the future, or a theory from the past that may project itself into the future, our imagination takes us out of the present and allows us the uniqueness of choice, something an animal does not have. This is the perfection I am talking about, desire is not wasted. It is still important to discipline ourselves through realizing the value of being in the present, because only then can we see our minds reacting. So you have a choice, you can become the ramifications of your desire or stand with your desire in the reality of being.

Survival

Seeing the law of survival strips away all the theological understandings, the different belief systems and faiths that have grown so thick over hundreds of years. The law of survival leaves us very naked indeed. But see the perfection of that nudity. It is by such an understanding that we survive. Then you can look at yourself and begin to realise what you really are and see your conditioning.

Acknowledgement of your conditioning will inevitably question the conclusions you draw, because you will see that your conditioning determines all your ideas of what life should be. Acknowledgement changes your ideas back to a much simpler observation of yourself. If I have a particular desire of experience, say for a peaceful, harmonious life, that is not acknowledging. Although being able to acknowledge your conditioning inevitably changes it, this change happens of its own accord; it is not something you seek or do. Therapists would say that if you are having psychological problems learn a different approach or do some in-depth analysis of your behaviour and then you won't have those problems. Doing this simply conforms to all your desires and so you are completely safe within your own identity. It is offering you utopia, nirvana, enlightenment. People come to me and say I need to meditate because I feel stressed, disharmonious, but that is seeing meditation as a therapy, a spiritual aspirin, and that is not what I'm talking about. The real question is "who" is needing to be humble, balanced, harmonious? Then you are challenging not just survival, but who is surviving. And it is a totally different thing to come to the realisation that there isn't anybody to survive.

The concept of survival I make light simply because I take the opposite as well. In seeing myself and each of you as fifteen-thousand million years old I am taking it fairly lightly. Am I taking the act of dying lightly? No, probably not. But then again, if you have already died it becomes quite a light thing. What causes the worry is fear for survival of death, that is the problem. I am saying mystics are free of that fear.

The reason you are serious is because survival demands the protection and continuation of "I". The dying here is the dying of "I". Now, don't confuse that with my survival. This is the crazy thing, if I'm hurting I will take an aspirin for I still suffer pain.

Lyn *To me it all seems mechanistic.*

No, it's not. The difference is I don't want any more of it than that; you do.

Lyn *What more do I want of it?*

A perpetuation of "I" beyond the experience itself.

Lyn *And are you saying with the death of the "I", there is no desire for more than the experience itself?*

It is not quite the death of "I" in the fatalistic way you are presenting it. It is the death of the ambition of "I". The ambition of "I" is my imagination projecting itself into some role or future ideal conditioned and conceptualized around my survival mechanism. There is an inability of the mind to accept the limitations of the simple principle of evolution. Is that all, you say to me? Yes, what's the problem? I am free of that problem; you are not, and there is the difference, that is all. Then you can be really light about it.

Survival is always about identity. It is always the mind that you are seeking to protect and to enable to survive because your mind is your identification. Until you can really grasp this you can't really tackle the whole essence of what we are doing here. It is not your physical survival we are challenging, we are challenging "you". Who are "you"? Just the slightest movement and the mind has got it – me, my identity. This is me understanding or not understanding, this is me being aggravated, this is me being happy. Who is understanding, aggravated, happy? That is the question, and it has got to be experiential, not simply a concept.

Mind always seeks a solution, and I am trying to show the motivation of survival itself. You are what you have made of that survival process, I am what I have made of that, and you need to understand that that process is uniquely you, and then simply to acknowledge it. I can acknowledge the perfection that is me, the perfection of my own ego. I am not going to resolve this. The real zen takes the movement itself and expands that movement into a living experience.

The Having Mode and Existential Being

Erich Fromm put the dilemma very clearly in his book, "To Have or to Be". He talks of two states, the having mode and existential being. Having things, what he calls the having mode, it seemed to him cannot buy one happiness. The normal state of the human being, he said, is existential being. He gives as examples of this state two children playing on the beach or a parent with their child; just relating to existence as it is, not demanding something of it.

Now I am not really sure that existential being is a natural thing; I almost think the having mode is part of our structure. I see it as the reverse. I think that we have to have things, that the having mode is part of our existence. It is the mode by which we survive. If existential being were the natural form for humans we would not have evolved, we would still be like the animals. The fact we are not appears to be because we have this incredible struggle of the having mode.

Mysticism, however, frees itself from the having mode and in a sense exists in existential being. By dropping the having mode I am free of my own personal ambition in relation to the total order of things. Existential being cannot be achieved through having. It is the having mode that demands an attachment or detachment; non-attachment doesn't. So happiness arises out of existential being, it is not something demanded; it is of itself. We can apply the same principle to what we are doing here. In as much as existential being is an experience with everything, identity clearly needs to be part of that – and indeed it is, and there is the paradox. Acknowledging that paradox is part of existential being, but it is not a demand of it. In the demand of it is the separation, which is okay too, because that is you, and that is part of existential being. It is the demand that separates us. The dynamic is that there is a detachment from this and there is an attachment to it, and that is how "I" survive. But existence is non-attachment, which is both of those but neither.

Freedom

What do I mean when I say freedom? Not an idea of freedom, a concept of freedom, not even a thought of freedom. The question I am posing is, can we be free of mind? Can we be free so completely that all that is present in the moment, in the now, is available to us? Do not make the mistake of thinking that the freedom I am talking about is a method, because it is not. Any method we employ would depend on an idea that we had, or something that we had learnt about in the past, someone else's idea of freedom, and that would be a distortion of reality, a limitation of the totality. It would be a limitation of the present by the desires our mind put on the place of now. So clearly we need a different approach to experience our life, for the freedom I am talking about cannot be learnt. It is, rather, a denial of the value of the reaction of mind as a solution of freedom.

The problem is you have made freedom a prisoner by your own demand of it. You see freedom as a goal and it is not. It is the opposite of what you believe. Freedom is; the goal is your problem. You don't have to attain freedom. Self-realization isn't something you attain, it is something you have. It becomes limited because you demand something of it.

If I can put in an idea of what this freedom is, or if I can put in the belief of what enlightenment is, call it what you like, we are quite happy to let go of all our other beliefs. But then you are left with your ideas of freedom, of enlightenment. This just replaces one set of values with another set of values, and then you find you are back where you started. It is the process that is the problem, not the set of values you pick up. But the only way you are prepared to let go of one set of values is if you find a better set that suits your conditioning. So what happens, and this is where it all gets very serious, is as you pull away those belief systems, as you scrape them off, you feel very vulnerable because you have got nothing to hang onto anymore. Your life, your survival is at stake here as far as you are concerned. You feel threatened because you are facing yourself.

There are many different analogies one can use. It is as if there are mirrors all around the edge of a table and I am an ant in the middle. These mirrors are closing in on me, so wherever I move I only see myself. That is a frightening experience. There comes the death of "I". But that death of "I" isn't how you imagine it. It is rather the death of the ambition for the death of "I". I have not met anybody yet who says they were very happy about this struggle, it seems to be a miserable experience. My own reaction was the worst three months of my life. What happened at the end of those three months was I let go of the cliff – and I didn't fall. And then you can have a good laugh.

I had to take on my whole ambition around this. I had heard these ideas of freedom, so what could possibly be the value of giving up something for absolutely nothing? That is how I saw it. We have got an idea of what freedom is. But the freedom I am talking about isn't an idea; it is an experience, an experiential relationship not a conceptual one.

Everything that we have deemed to be important in our lives, maybe even our spiritual search, we have achieved by thought and memory motivated by our desires. But this freedom I am talking about is free of thought, free of memory and free of desire. Yet within our minds all desire is thought, thoughts recalled from memory. Mind itself is thought, the process of memory and desire. "I" am thought.

Leading neurologists recently have suggested that "I" or self is an illusion. Mystics have always said that. Clearly that thought of "I" is how I know I exist. But can I exist without the need to have a desire of the experience or even the memory of past experiences? In other words can I have an experience with the present without the need to change it with my desire or rely on my memory to interpret it – is that possible?

To do so I clearly must have a thought, a reaction to the present, or I would not know I existed. Supposing as I react to the present I place no value on that reaction, I have no desire for the reaction to be any different than it really is. My reaction then to experience would not need to be limited by the mind's idea of that experience and I would be free to simply just experience the present. But as soon as I react with an object and name that object from my memory I limit the present to the name I call that object – table, chair, tree, whatever it may be. Clearly a reaction must happen in this process because reaction is me, "I", and without a reaction I would have no sense of identity with the present at all. "I" would simply cease to exist.

The senses, which feed the brain are always open to everything. The eyes see, the ears hear, the hands touch. This in reality is the beginning and end of it. It is the mind that makes something of what they see, it is the mind that makes something of what they hear, it is the mind that makes something of what they touch. "I" am the process that limits that openness and creates an identity. So when J. Krishnamurti asked the question, "Can the brain be open to everything?" the answer is, "Yes, it always is." It is the mind that limits you, but that limit is needed in order that "I" can create an identity and a separation from existence. The only limit that exists is the limit created by your mind, including its ideas of what totality, reality and existence mean.

Is there a moment in which everything is? No, everything is in the moment, and there is a big difference. The moment is what you have made of it. If everything is one, then you are part of everything. The moment doesn't hold everything; you have made a moment of everything. It is quite perfect; it is quite beautiful. Freedom is where mind demands nothing of the everything of the experience.

The way the mind creates separation is by the process of what in Buddhism is called the three facets of ego – identity, possessiveness and ambition. For me ego is principally about an identification of self, it is about the survival of the individual, and to augment that survival, it seems to me, we are both possessive and ambitious of our own demands of life. I cannot overcome that process, but I do not need to make it a limit. The realisation that "I" is a process of limiting life into fragments – past, present, and future; right and wrong; happiness and unhappiness; ambition and non ambition; good and bad; and so on – that "I" am such a limitation, is an incredibly profound understanding. It is also incredibly simple; it is not difficult.

We have to avoid making a method out of not limiting it, because any method will become a limitation. But neither can "I" realise totality by being less limited because "I" is a reaction, and reaction is always limited to its demand of existence. This is why I argue that enlightenment is a limitation, because enlightenment is a demand of the experience in accordance with your expectation of it. Whereas self-realisation is the realisation that you inevitably limit existence, so "I" am always relative to my demand of existence. Then you can acknowledge the perfection of this limitation and the relative position I am talking about, because it is how you know yourself.

The name we give to this reaction is duality, it is how I separate myself from totality. Reaction is duality at work. Reaction is how "I" exists. "I" can only exist in duality, "I" cannot exist outside of duality. When thought ceases "I" ceases to be separate, but then "I" also ceases to be aware of the separation. So I can never overcome duality because I am duality. The ultimate question then is: does an awareness exist beyond "I"? Yes, but "I" cannot have it. How do I know that? "I" do not.

Let me explain. It does not matter what we call this awareness because that is just another name the mind has raised. I call it existence, "a plurality of consciouness", others call it God, everything, totality; but these are all just words. In this existence, this awareness, nothing is separate, nothing. There is no future, no past, there is no right, no wrong. Rather there is all future, all past; there is all right, all wrong. There is no judgement, there is all judgements. There is no "I", there is all "I"s. Duality is the illusion that creates the reaction.

It is not a state you can describe, so mystics say it cannot be said. This is where the riddle of the thing comes in, because when you try to explain it you find yourself claiming it. You find yourself claiming it either as being full or being empty, and "I" can't really do that. So how do I portray this sense of totality? Well this is the age-old mystical problem. It doesn't bear a definition, and if you look at 'The Great Way' and its attempt to actually state it, you will see that the contradiction is covered each time by Seng-ts'an. He is not able simply to say I am feeling empty or I am feeling nothing, because if I am feeling empty then that is the opposite of feeling full. Similarly he does not call it one, because in saying it is one creates an idea of one. So mystics in their wisdom say not two, "I" and everything else. In this way they come to the amazing understanding that in the whole universe there is only one duality, you and the universe. Nothing else is separate, only the reaction of "I" as mind.

Truth is, with no thought. I can no longer separate truth into something, and if I do it is simply a relative truth of my mind. It is "I" that makes relative truth, it is "I" that determines what truth is, truth that is made up by "I". You come to the realisation that there is no way you can think your way to this freedom because thought cannot produce freedom.

You also realise, as J. Krishnamurti said, that there are not different levels of thought. There are no holy thoughts greater than lesser thoughts, no superior, no inferior thoughts, there is only the process of thinking. It is not as if thoughts of God are higher in some way, as if some mantra we could think up and start chanting could take us somewhere nearer totality than the thoughts of our day-to-day life. The day-to-day life is where it happens, the reality of our experience is the closest we can get to it. When we think we are nearer God, it is only a thought of being nearer God, it is not the experience. Making some thoughts more divine than others simply meets the desires of our mind, because the freedom I am talking about, the freedom of totality exists beyond all thought.

What is a "plurality of consciousness" that does not think? The experience of the thought of you is how consciousness knows itself. You suddenly become aware that if duality truly is an illusion, your reaction is God, everything, totality knowing itself. The mystical state is that only one duality exists as an illusion, you and the experience itself, there is nothing else. It is a paradox that cannot be resolved, so why try? Our minds, because of ego's need for identity and for survival, seem to have an insatiable need to resolve this paradox. But the mystical experience is beyond mind.

Who or what can experience something beyond mind? A consciousness that is present in everything but cannot be identified separately in anything, because any separate identification becomes a limitation like table, chair, me, you and so on. There is a force that seems to manifest as a need to evolve, that seems to exist in our very genetic structure. Osho speaks of a knowing in which there is no knower. It is not a knowing of thought, not a knowing of mind. It is a knowing born of movement, a knowing born of experience, of evolution, of God, all meaningless names that we give it. That knowing, that movement has a consciousness of itself and that consciousness is us. It is not you, it is not me, it is us.

This "plurality of consciousness" is where the observer and the observed are not divided by thought, which is "I". When I am no longer separate as "I", when duality in other words is not two, the brain is open to everything, the perceptive senses are open to everything. Mind has then ceased to react to everything, so no thought of something exists. "I" has become the experience by reacting to everything and not to something.

This is the mystical experience, experiencer and experience are indivisible. "I" has nothing to gain and rests in totality, and not in duality. "I" has become a plurality because it has no demand or desire of the experience other than what is. And a separation from that plurality can only occur if "I" has a desire out of everything called something. "I" dissolves into brain's openness to everything. Brain is one with being. The perceptive senses are open, but the brain does not respond as a reaction of mind. To respond would define a separation and an identity with "I" as a reaction.

Duality has ceased, time no longer exists, knowing is absorbed in the perfection of movement. Happiness, fear, judgment, life is seen from a totality not from a separation. "I" is reacting, that is how I know I exist, but "I" is reacting out of knowing, not survival. The mystic is all that she or he has always been, still with their identity, with their ego. Nothing has really changed, but when you understand the perfection of the process there is no need for change.

The Nature of Opposites.

Let us examine the nature of opposites within experience. The law of opposites, for instance, is that by having a desire not to have a desire we create another desire. How can we not do that? If you make it joy you make it hate, that is simply just the opposite state. The experience occurs neither in joy nor in hate or anger. You begin to understand that this law of opposites in nature must apply to every experience. The mystic experience sees the totality of opposites, with no separation. As one person said to me once, they could suddenly see both sides of the coin at the same time. Yes, but then there is a reaction to that and there's another line drawn. We are the reaction; we can never be anything but the reaction. It is a paradox, it cannot be resolved.

MATTHEW *That has been part of my struggle the last two weeks, trying to figure out whether I am the reaction or the experience. And maybe the experience is the reaction. Basically, Who is the acknowledger? In every situation, moment to moment, I have a reaction. But then I wonder am I just the reaction to that experience? For some reason I can't put my finger on, I found it very unsettling trying to struggle with, "Am I the experience?" and then sensing that there is no separation between me and the experience; that it is all the same thing. It feels like my nose nudging up against the paradox that there is a separate identity and yet we are all one. I find it very frustrating, because it looks as if I will never know who I am other than simply as the reaction to what happened just the moment before. So it is as if I am always one step behind the experience.*

Why you are frustrated is because you want something from it; you have a desire of this outside of the experience of it. Why shouldn't you experience frustration when you are trying to achieve something that you are not? So you are a frustrated person; what's the big deal? In that you begin to understand what is happening. How else would you be but frustrated, what would you expect to be any different? There lies the key.

MATTHEW *But nonetheless I want it to be different. If I look at it dispassionately I wouldn't expect it to be anything other than frustrating, and yet I do want it to be different. I want it to be harmonious.*

And there lies the opposite; that is the line you are drawing isn't it? The more you try to make it harmonious, the more you get the opposite.

This work challenges every avenue of escape, so you are getting into smaller and smaller places. This is the analogy of the mirrors that are constantly closing in on the ant on the table top; what's happening is gradually the mirrors are moving in. The experience, if you listen to every mystic throughout time, is that there is no answer. It is this realisation that awakens you. The koan is aimed to develop the paradox of opposites to a crisis.

The frustration of the inability to identify yourself can also show itself by shouting and screaming. Doing this again reinforces very strongly the identity which has been held back. It is important not to hold back. There is nothing wrong with shouting, with being bad tempered, it is you. The freedom comes out of acknowledging that this is how you are, of not having a stereotype of how you should be – sort of floating two feet off the ground, chanting om, completely at peace. It's not about that, it is all about identity and survival.

PAT *Wouldn't you want to hold the frustration in so that you explode your concepts. The frustration is there to be built up so that you break through.*

Who's going to break through the frustration if the frustration itself is you?

It is a valid question you are asking and people get to that point and then they have got no answer. Who is being frustrated? Frustration is seen as being something separate from you, but you are the frustration. "I" is the frustration.

The frustration is an impediment, a hindrance in good old Buddhist terminology. Frustration is an indication that your state of mind, by its nature, is a limitation. Frustration is defining your desire of that experience, which is all it is doing. But you are that desire of the experience. Now one could argue that if you worked with this you would become less frustrated. So then you simply identify yourself as being a less frustrated individual rather than a more frustrated individual; so what?

This is something that is really not approached in spiritual work and mysticism; it's just glossed over. We have this idea that we should live in a sort of harmonious equilibrium, free of all hindrances, in complete passivity, and that is where it happens. No, no. That is not to say being harmonious, equanimous and non-frustrated is not a desirable thing. Of course it is. For years I worked at the practice of meditation to master becoming less frustrated. It's wonderful, it's beautiful, but it has absolutely nothing to do with mysticism. From my point of view, to see vipassana in this way is to see it as a therapy tool, probably one of the best. But what is being said here is that it isn't about therapy, about becoming not frustrated. It is about blowing the identity itself. Then who is left?

You are desperately trying to identify something which can be you that isn't a concept. But you are your concepts. In this case the concept is frustration. Every concept you form, every thought you have, every act you take, inevitably creates its opposite.

What you are feeling is this incredible dilemma because our whole genetic structure is programmed to survive, to find something for me. "What's in this for me?" is the constant question self asks, and I am offering self, "me", nothing. I am offering it oblivion. Your identity demands a method to reach the mystical experience. So I give Matthew a method to do it and Matthew goes away and does this method, and what happens is he gets more and more frustrated. Why shouldn't he? He is bound to because there is actually nothing in this for him. The experience of life is everything, not something.

Experientially it is a relationship that most of you in this room have had and have attempted to identify and label and idealize. I am simply saying the act of doing so is an act of separation from it. So the dilemma is that at some point you have got to acknowledge that the experience of everything cannot be resolved in terms of identity and survival. It cannot be because it is not about survival. What you are dealing with is that the mind is a process of reducing everything down to something and that something gives you an identity called Pat, for example, which ensures that Pat survives, because without that identity she couldn't survive. That is the process of mind that is Pat. But it is only a concept that there is something else there other than this process in the mind. It is only a concept that a separate self exists, although one that Pat is quite happy with because it gives her a continuity of identity after she dies. That same motivation exists on a day-to-day basis constantly. But the experience of mysticism doesn't have some value called reincarnation, soul, higher self. The experience of mysticism is all value, including every feeling – frustration, anger, joy – and you can't make anything of all value anymore than you can make anything of everything.

The mystical experience is a totality; it encompasses all opposites so you can't subdivide it up. Immediately you make a higher self you make a no-higher self. Immediately you make God you make no-God. How you survive is by limiting everything down into something – an ideology, a belief system, or whatever it may be. But experience is all of those beliefs, not one of them, and it is all of no-belief too. It is everything, it is the whole universe, it has no limit.

Now am I saying that the human brain can react to this limitless everything? Yes, I am saying that; so there is a positiveness. Am I saying that my mind can react to all value? Yes, I am saying that. But it has no value to me unless "I"- the self, the mind, the person who answers to a certain name, who believes he or she has a past history and a future one – can make some value of it.

At this point there is a value that motivates me and motivates others like me, and that motivation is called freedom. It is the freedom from having to make some value of it. You are free from the desire to make something for yourself out of this – called nirvana, heaven, joy, bliss, ecstasy, love, whatever. Life is simply the experience itself within the perfection of itself, which is everything and has all value.

We can say that in the frustration that builds up there is an objective. The objective is to be free, but not to have an idea of what that freedom is, for that would be somewhere for self to hide. Freedom is not like you imagine it. As long as you can make something of it you have got an identity and you have a separation. What I say is just my unique relationship to it, neither right nor wrong. I haven't got the answers here because as long as you can judge what I am saying you still have an identity.

The famous saying that "if you are a Buddhist, you are not one" indicates that it isn't a conceptual value of Buddhism, it isn't a method of Buddhism. And you can take away the Buddha and put anything there. You could put me there, and then you have to kill me for you have got to get past my concepts. The key in the ideas that you are given here lies in their relationship to your own experience and to the way you separate that experience off.

The motivation that is driving you forward is something that is genetic, deep within you. It is searching for a way to find God and resolve God. I call it God because I don't know what else to call it. It is a total part of my nature; it is how God knows itself. I am not an atheist but neither am I searching anymore. Now I don't know whether the frustration you drive yourself into in a koan changes something physically or chemically in the brain, whether maybe the so-called God-spot is burnt out. I really don't know, but something has changed. Now that is a change I am saying of freedom as an experience, not as a concept.

For some a religious faith, Christian, Islamic, Buddhist, whatever, seems to satisfy that need. For many others such beliefs don't work very well. But that need is still there, and what you have to do in this work is to actually face the need itself, not its solution. And that means looking at your motivation. Why am I searching and what do I need from this? What this throws up challenges your survival. That is where the frustration arises, but the act of acknowledgment takes out the intensity. Desire is only a problem at the moment, that is all. It is like a passing thought. I am just frustrated, the frustration is my experience, it's me, and there is no problem. It's not that I shouldn't be frustrated, no, no.

Go back to the wisdom of Seng-ts'an, the third Chinese Zen patriarch, when he says, "make the slightest preference and you are an infinite distance apart." Do I express preferences? You bet I do. But on the other hand they have gone. So here is the paradox: on the one hand I haven't changed a bit, I am just the same person that I ever was, but all the same something is free from the need to resolve my survival, to resolve who I am. Freedom itself exists in the motivation, not the solution. It is freedom as an experience, not as a conceptual thing.

Whatever the experience is let us not define it, because it becomes simply a concept if we do. The freedom I am talking about isn't a conceptual realisation; it is being free of the need to make something out of it, to make some value of it. I am free of having concepts in the sense that I acknowledge their limitation; the experience is quite perfect as it is.

Identity

Eckhart said, "God has nothing more to do in you." Such a statement requires an incredible surrender. It makes an immediate challenge to your identity and purpose in life, the need for self to identify itself somewhere within the process of life. The very act of surrender itself has implications of separation. Often it is interpreted as surrendering my identity or surrendering myself. But what is being surrendered? Who is surrendering? What you have to acknowledge is that the act of surrender is neither about surrendering nor is it about identity.

Whatever force we create we automatically create an opposite force, and if we see surrender as the opposite to identity that is virtually the flip side of the same coin.

I can accept that I don't really need to identify myself, and that what happens in the thinking process is that there are still bits of me grabbing on there. But neither can I talk about surrender, because what's going to surrender if that isn't another method, another process. You can begin to see both sides of this. Neither side is right or wrong, but both are a separation away from the place where the experience is, which is in the actual movement of the experience itself.

The surrender that I'm talking of is about not needing to identify. It's not about giving up identity. There is a huge difference. If you don't **need** to identify, you don't have to give up identity. So in the quietude of now I don't say, look, I'm here. Nor do I say the opposite, look, I give up 'I'm here', for this is really just the same thing. There is a very subtle place here that is inclusive and is neither of the opposites. You begin to get a hint of the Buddha's middle way.

Looking at it in terms of attachment, detachment and non-attachment, surrender is actually non-attachment, the surrendering of my need to be attached. Attachment has as its opposite detachment, not non-attachment. Non-attachment means I don't have to be attached, for who is needing to be attached? But that doesn't mean I'm going to be detached.

It's a very subtle thing but it's incredibly important in our work, because it allows us to stand within the freedom from **needing** an identity. It doesn't mean that identity won't occur. I still have an identity and I am still relating to it. But it is a place to be aware of. It is an acknowledgement that you are still thinking at least the one thought of awareness, because even awareness or observing is a thought. Observer and observed define a subjective place: I the observer observing. It is very tentative, just being aware at the moment, just being aware of the reaction of mind within the experience itself. But that is the beginning and end of it.

I am aware that I am having a reaction to an experience and at the same time I let it go. Not that there is a place for it to go. There isn't an augmentation of identity, there isn't a reinforcing of views, of belief systems. There isn't seen to be a progression or method that is going forward. It is just simply standing in that space, in that experience. The subtlety of this is quite amazing.

What quietude does, if you are aware enough, is it enables you to actually see the identity within the smallest movement of yourself. Look immediately towards the motive of every action you do, don't look for its solution. It is not a question of being wrong and there is no need to change what you do. It is simply acknowledging and being able to observe the constant identity we make within the experience of life itself. It is a constant movement that has to be understood and accepted.

What you find is that self really has got nowhere to move. Self looks for a positive identity, a harmonious, balanced place where it would like to be. But there is no difference, in terms of my identity and separation from experience, between a harmonious place and my walking through the door and shouting at everybody. Certainly to walk in chanting om may give my words greater credibility with you because that's infinitely more peaceful, more passive, more gentle, more humble and you attribute that behaviour to be a consequence of my experience. It is nothing of the sort; it is still a separation from my experience. Who said that an angry man cannot be a mystic? What has anger or lack of anger got to do with being a mystic? What have moral values got to do with totality? Doesn't mysticism include all values? You can see how many ideas we have around what a mystic is, how we have expectations of how a mystic should be – a shaven head, special clothes. If I'm not big enough to see how I am playing games with my identity then I'm going to get hooked into my ideas of what a mystic should be, and that will become my separation.

Mysticism means an absolute surrender to experience as it exists. Moral judgements exist as a consequence of social behaviour but not as a consequence of everything. By an experience of everything why should I become more morally right or wrong in anyone's eyes? This is a big challenge to all the ideas that we have of this space.

Always look, it needs to be underlined, at the motivation of the way we sit, the way we talk, our every gesture. Everything has a significance, nothing is wasted, nothing. The key is in your reaction. That is the place where your growth lies, that is the place of challenge. All you can do is to watch. It's standing in that place and just allowing the situation to happen and just watching what happens within your mind, there is nothing needed outside of that. This endless movement inward will throw up all sorts of things, and what we are talking about here is the freedom from the need to resolve anything.

What is offered here is the freedom from the process of having to make an identity. I am simply saying that your identity is your reaction to life, and that is all there is. I could say I'm a Master, I'm a Teacher, I'm a humorous person, I could make a thousand different definitions about who I am. But to me there is no separation. "I" includes everything. Identity simply means everything that you associate with being you. Your genetics, conditioning, everything, because if we seek to divide it up, the more confusing you can make it, the more opportunity you have got for self to escape into some concept, into someone else's idea of a soul, of a higher self. I have found everything and I have found something called identity, and identity is me, my thinking process. I haven't got a relationship with anything else.

I begin to see that identity can change from moment to moment. It can be lover, it can be teacher, it can be healer, it can be writer, cook. And as it changes its role it reinforces what self believes is a multi-role existence. But that isn't the experience that I have; it is just my idea of it, an illusion of a separate self. When I really work it down I have a thought of cooking, I have a thought of writing, I have a thought of teaching, and I rely on my brain and its memory banks to augment and supplement that to give it credibility. The only experience I am is my reaction to life, which is all of those ideas of a separate self.

Now we must be very careful not to slip in another identity called religious experience or spiritual experience or Being or Self and give that a greater priority than we would being a chef, for example. The challenge of that is incredible. There isn't a Being there, it's just being in the moment, with a small b, just being a reaction. To define some separate place that is different from the thinking process is how an illusion of self is created.

MATTHEW *There was a point in a session with David recently when I realized that I'm just a thought changing; new thought, new thought, new thought. I had an experience, a sense that all there is is a bunch of thoughts changing – and that that is a thought also.*

This is what I mean by kensho, meaning an experience in which there is no separate self, where self is seen to be an integral part, not separate. It is an experience, not a belief system, that denies the existence of a separate self. Why you need a belief system is in order to maintain and perpetuate the illusion of a separate self. It is vitally important for you to do that, because if you have got a separate self, call it Being, call it soul, whatever you want to call it, then you can retain an identity and a purpose in your existence.

It might seem that without an identity and a purpose your life would be totally wasted. The reality is that kensho produces a freedom from that need for such purpose. The experience is rich, but it is not rich in relationship to life but in itself. There is a perfection in life as it is; it doesn't need a separate Being, a separate Self, a soul, or anything else. Consciousness to me is simply a subjective process which is called "I", the process that identifies a relationship with the experience.

LINDSEY *I'm noticing anger within myself recently and I am wondering why there is anger when you get to the depths of this?*

I wouldn't expect your reaction to be anything else because I am really challenging your whole identity, your whole survival. You see when I talk about it being the ultimate human experience, it is also the ultimate human challenge. There's no messing about with this, this is right down where it hurts. This is where the mind forms an identity and I am threatening that. Hence people are going to become angry, that's their way out of it. Don't underestimate the force of this, because people kill each other for things like this, just look at fundamentalism.

It is even better in many ways to be angry than peaceful. If you are sitting in complete harmony with me a certain motive has been lost. What a friend you have in your anger. Part of you is saying I shouldn't be feeling angry. Why not? But on the other hand, if Jo, for instance, were feeling very harmonious with what I am saying, there can still be just as much growth there as in feeling anger because the question would then be, why the feeling of harmony?

JO *But it's harder for self if it's harmonious because self doesn't want to move out of that space. But self definitely wants to move out of the angry space or the upset space.*

And why this is so is because anger is seen as a threat to survival, whereas harmony is seen as complementary to survival. I am constantly creating my relationship with the experience that is around me, creating a sense of survival out of it.

The second aspect of vipassana is to go back each time to the experience, to the origin of the thought itself. This is exactly what we should be doing experientially as we are working with life. As I react to a tree, that thought gives rise to another thought of some other tree, which is perhaps becoming a danger to my house, and so there is the thought that I need to do something. Before I know where I am I have lost the experience around me and I have gone off miles into the future thinking about the security of my home. What you have to do is retrace your steps, exactly the same as if you were sitting. As you train the mind you can pick up on it quicker. I'll pick up on a run and immediately I am right back in the present with the experience again.

Gradually you polish the mirror and suddenly you become aware of how you are working. You also begin to acknowledge the perfection of that. We are not talking about being correct; it's not right or wrong to feel harmonious or angry, it's not right or wrong to have judgements. As you become aware of how you work you become aware of the perfection of it, and as you become aware of the perfection of it you will find it will change – since everything is in change.

This is the power of acknowledgement, because as I've always said don't worry about what you are doing just acknowledge it. You can take hold of your life and actually see what is going on. Then you begin to recognize the perfection of anger because you are not caught in it, you are simply standing and watching it happen. And as you begin to recognize the perfection of anger you will find that you use it less. But don't see this as a method of overcoming anger, because it's not.

To say you shouldn't be angry, or you need to express your anger and then you will find harmony, because harmony is where you want to be – to say that is therapy. I am not saying that, I am not talking therapy here. I am saying that anger is a perfectly natural expression of you, there's nothing wrong with it at all. And so indeed is harmony. You are angry or you are harmonious because you have a desire of experience and either it is complying with your desire of it or it is not. If it is not complying with your desire you are angry, if it is you are happy or harmonious. If I walk out of my front door in the morning and I feel complete harmony with life, that's the way it is. If I walk out in the morning and I feel complete anger with life, that's the way it is. There is no right or wrong in it; it just is like that. Suddenly there is an acceptance of the experience.

Watch the mind, and as you watch the mind you know you have gone to one extreme or its opposite, into happiness or misery. There is a place where you can begin to see the nature of the desire entering into experience itself and separating you from experience, you can actually see it happening. Now that is being awake. It is being awake to the expectation you are putting on the relationship with a person, or on any environment you find yourself in at any given moment.

If you pick up on any one of those at sufficient depth, you will go straight back to survival. Out of survival there is a need for identity, and for possession and ambition which reinforce identity. Nothing is wrong, nothing needs to be changed. Everything exists in every moment, it never does not exist. And the only way you can have an identity of everything is to bring it back to something, and that something can be anger or harmony or benevolence or even a sense of Being. It is all exactly the same, it is all about identity.

The mystical experience exists, it isn't something you attain. It is permanent, it is here now, it exists in this very room, it exists with every moment of your consciousness. The mystical experience is an experience of freedom from wanting something from it; and the freedom of wanting something from it is everything, because you have not reduced it to a benefit – to something called satori, enlightenment, peace, etc. And it doesn't mean you change. So you can begin to see the wisdom of Ram Dass when he says he hasn't really changed. Why should he?

Kensho can't be defined. It is a relationship with everything which essentially doesn't demand anything other than the experience itself. But there is still a relationship there of self existing because self is reacting to experience. Whereas in having an enlightenment experience there is nothing stopping one still retaining a value in that like love, ecstasy, bliss; but that isn't kensho.

The nature of self has to be understood as being an illusion of separation, but only an illusion can benefit from an illusion. Unless I have got an illusion of self, I can't benefit from it.

DEVO *But can you ever be free of making limitations out of experience?*

I'm saying yes, you can be free of the need to make a limitation, but not of making one. You need to make a limitation of this, I don't. But that doesn't mean I don't make my own limitation; I make a limitation, but I don't **need** to make it, because I don't have a need for an identity. I am my identity, I don't need more. I do need an identity to survive, which is, why I create one, but not because I need to. Whereas you do it because you need to do it.

TANYA *What is the difference?*

MATTHEW *The difference is in motivation. The outcome is identical, the juice is in motivation. The motivation for you perhaps is the fear of death because you think Tanya exists. Whereas the motivation for David, who doesn't fear death, is because he knows that David doesn't exist. And that is fundamental. The motivation for you is the fact that somewhere there is a Tanya saying she exists and she doesn't want to die. So you need to survive and identify, whereas I presume why David says he doesn't need to survive is because somewhere he knows he doesn't exist. So whether he lives or dies isn't important, and yet the genetic structure of his body-mind has him eat, sleep, walk, and survive and die. The gestalt is utterly different.*

Thank you Matthew that is very clearly put.

TANYA *So for you David you just live. For me there is a need behind my living.*

And the reason the need has ceased for me is because kensho showed me as an experience that no separate self existed. The need dies with that. So I am free from the need for self to exist separately.

TANYA *So you no longer have the need to exist because you have had the experience where you didn't feel separate from everything, you were one with it.*

MATTHEW *Not you were one with it, it was. You are immediately creating a Tanya and it. It was. There is a massive difference. There wasn't David doing anything with anybody.*

Thank you again Matthew. It's impossible really to convey. We can only confirm what it isn't, because the self's expression will always have a limit, so it's not that, it's not that, *netti, netti*. It is not the limit, Matthew, that you and I are putting on it now, but how else do we approach it. I mean the brilliant talk you have given isn't the answer, that is the limit you have placed on it.

MATTHEW *The sense I get from our talks is that often we are all very busy with the screen and what comes to me is what's driving the projector, how is the projector functioning? What is moving the projector? What I find myself very busy with a lot, is what the screen is showing me instead of what is making the projector move. That seems to be more where the key lies in who I am.*

To me, using your analogy, the only value the screen has is in my being able to identify myself as being separate, the nature of my reaction, because the screen doesn't really exist until I see it; if I don't see it, it doesn't exist. I reclaim identity by the ability to see things, to hear things, to touch things. And that's my process, which is all I am, I don't need any more than that.

MATTHEW *But what is occurring to me is the red-herringness of all of it, and what I mean by the red-herringness of it is that this doesn't mean anything; it is just as it is, there really is no answer. There is nothing to change, there's no juice in it, there is no significance in it; it's just as it is, and so what.*

And that in itself is beautiful and wonderful and incredible and awesome. Krishnamurti gives a clue when he says, "the more the tree is like a tree, the more it is like God."

MATTHEW *Then it shines in itself, then it's pure. I get it, I understand.*

There is no limit to the tree, only what you make it. The paradox is that even though you define human beings as being everything, humans are designed to separate themselves. We can't do anything but that. When I began with Eckhart's phrase, "God has nothing more to do in you", it is exactly the same as J. Krishnamurti saying, "the more the tree is like a tree the more it is like God." There really is no difference in the two expressions, they are exactly the same thing. In other words, the experience is as it is.

Kensho

"Kensho. Japanese meaning literally "seeing nature." Zen expression for the experience of awakening, usually translated as "self-realization." The experience contains no duality of "seer" and "seen" because there is no "nature of self" as an object that is seen by a subject separate from it. Although kensho and satori are often used synonymously, it is customary to use the word satori for the enlightenment of the Buddha and the Zen patriarchs and kensho for the initial enlightenment experience that still requires to be deepened.

(The Rider Encyclopedia of Eastern Philosophy and Religion, 1989)

There isn't such a thing as *kensho*, that is just a name I found and have given to something that happened for several of us – as a consequence of our creation of it. So do not start with an ambition of what enlightenment, *kensho* is; all I have said of *kensho* is that it is a realization that no separate self exists, full stop. I haven't said it's got anything. Now that immediately confronts your ambition of it because your ambition wants to make it bliss, happiness, peace, a whole host of things. So *kensho*, enlightenment becomes very ordinary, lacks ambition, lacks anything to possess. It is intended to, because if you place an ambition into *kensho* or a possessiveness into it you will surely find only what you yourself have put into it.

The experience we are talking of here is not an experience of limitation; it is an experience of no limit. You are the limitation you make of that experience. Before that experience can happen it appears that you have to blow away the limitations that you are seeking of it. When you no longer seek to place your own identity in an object, what's called subjective consciousness, then experience starts to come to you, which is termed objective awareness. But any reaction you make of that experience will always be its limit – called enlightenment, satori, nirvana, even *kensho*.

The Unsayable: Hossen

"Hossen is the exchange of words, questions and answers between two enlightened people"

In our work we are moving towards the zen of understanding the contradiction, the paradox. We started from the premise that really there is no separate self to experience life, and now we are going further than this. The more I am working with this experience the more I'm realizing that all the things I had attributed to a mystical place could in fact be within the movement of my own mind, the product of conditioning. What I am left with, it seems to me, is an experience which I can't explain because the very explanation of it is a limitation. That mystical experience is what is present in every moment of the day, but immediately it attempts to take some shape or form I find myself in a place of relying on my own conditioned interpretation.

Zen says it is words beyond words. But what does that mean? It is experience beyond the direct relationship of life as we know it, but what does that mean? It is paradoxical, but what does that mean? It is ambiguous, it is contradictory, it is dialectical, but what do all those expressions mean? What do they mean in terms of my own relationship with the mystical experience itself? What is my relationship with the universe as I now see it? As I take away my limitations an experience broadens, but that experience is not definable in any way that makes sense. And as I evolve in my interpretation I find my interpretation becoming extremely limited, almost mundane even.

My role in our discussions together, as I've always said, is reflective, an attempt to polish the mirror. After a while you begin to question why you are looking in the mirror, and the reason you are looking in the mirror is the reason why you have come here. In your minds you are here for some desire of this, some expectation of this, some demand of it. So I'm busy polishing the mirror each time and holding it up and saying there you are, and I might twist it a little bit, and you say yes, you see. But what are you looking for? What are you seeking to achieve in the reflection? Isn't the same limitation I am talking about now revealing itself in our work together?

It is very interesting to watch several people who are coming back to me with interpretations of kensho because they are becoming confused themselves about what they want from coming here. Inevitably this must be so, because in a way what is happening is they are undressing their very core relationship to survival and to existence. So all the desires to be here have to be looked at and understood and challenged. Not to define them as being right or wrong, but to challenge them by looking at them from the point of view of their authenticity in relation to our life.

One of the greatest dilemmas I have faced in my work has been the relationship of mind and its survival to our "existential" need. I believe that there is what could be called a need of "existence" deep within us, which is almost genetic. This "existential" need is only seen as being part of our normal survival activity because we haven't acknowledged it as being something that is already built within us. Survival has no place within this need of "existence". What happens is that up until the point of realization that self isn't separate, self behaves separately in demanding from its survival mechanism that it should be satisfied "existentially". But the realization of kensho throws the mind into a dilemma because although the motivation is still there, there is no self needing to experience it. Our only motivation now should really be this genetic need within us. You are free of the **need** to experience it, and I underline the need as a desire, as a demand. Now this dilemma has to be acknowledged. If you don't acknowledge it then you tie it in to all your normal survival activities. But if the "existential" need is genetic within us it doesn't bear a relationship to self. It is the need of "existence" rather, the genetic need of the universe.

The reason I have separated the two types of need is to show that when you do something about survival you then become free of the genetic need to resolve life, the "existential" genetic need. But that does not mean that the genetic need to understand existence doesn't still exist, and here the paradox arises. In kensho one arrives at a place free of the need of self to resolve life. But then one finds oneself asking what purpose is there, for example, in coming here to Peacefields, because until now every structured activity that has existed within one's life has been dependent on the self surviving.

The confusion arises because people have experienced the nature of no self yet at the same time they are still finding that the motive of trying to understand the purpose, the meaning of existence, is still present within the brain itself. I think that is part of the genetic response of human kind, part of the original need of the universe. This means that it is outside the origins of my own conditioning. We can try to explain that in terms of survival – but then it becomes very difficult to see why my survival should be dependent on me knowing God.

MATTHEW *But why lump that into DNA to validate it for that could be as illusory as the next thing?*

Because not to do so would define that there was some external influence of which I am not part. What else could motivate you if it wasn't DNA, genetic? Otherwise you start to believe in the idea of some mystical force of which you have no experience. In doing this you give away the credibility of your own direct relationship with it.

What I am trying to do is to bring the experience of no self back to a practical reality within your own experience. I am trying to take away the mystical relationship to it.

The reason I am needing to do that constantly is because as I do so I find that there is more and more validity in such a movement as an experience. If I turn around and say that those motivations exist as some force that is out there I immediately abrogate any responsibility in myself for that relationship. If I say that the experience of no self is up to me, that it is part of my movement, my design, my relationship to life, then it becomes more tangible and easier to work with. I am trying to bring it into a more practical, positive relationship with my own life and my own mind. As I do that the mystical place of it expands, but not in terms of an identifiable experience of which I am part.

MATTHEW *So the mystical experience expands, but the mystic doesn't.*

Exactly. In fact if anything he or she diminishes. What actually started off as a great big thing for me is getting less and less in terms of me but the experience itself is getting greater and greater. Once you take all the externalities away and you come down to the kernel of the relationship between yourself and the universe you begin to see that it is a very simple and a very dynamic thing. It doesn't require all the dressing you have given it before because you are free of demanding self out of it, you are free of making something for yourself out of that relationship.

Even though it may not sound very exciting, I find it more exciting in a way because it is bringing a practical, almost a touchable thing within my life. I think if you can acknowledge that touchable thing you don't then have to be trapped by it. You can still carry on moving through as long as you hold the origin and you are big enough to be able to change your mind, big enough not to try to hold a place where it exists. Then all the experiences that you have had or believed you have had in your life throw themselves into the cauldron and you need to sort them out.

What I am saying here isn't really in any contradiction with what I used to say, but it is becoming more definitive because the mystical aspects of it have a credible relationship with my experience of life. Really they are not mystical at all, they are simply mechanical in relation to the state of mysticism.

So what do I now see mysticism as? For me mysticism is an extra-dimensional relationship that the brain is capable of experiencing; and that is all. Anything I make of that relationship will be my limit of it. And I see that extra-dimensional relationship as tied in absolutely with everything that exists. Paradox only occurs when you try to make three dimensions of something that is greater. Going back to my analogy of a two-dimensional man, the two-dimensional line can never have a three-dimensional relationship; it is necessarily limited by its own perception. My human brain relates with my mind, the movement of brain being mind, in a three-dimensional plane, but the brain does seem to be capable of an extra-dimensional experience. The problem is "I" can't make anything of that, and as I give up the need to make something of that I begin to realize the perfection of my own mind in relation to the third dimension in which I live.

MATTHEW *In my experience it is not that I can't make anything of it, it is that I can't communicate it, I can't express it. But I can make something of it because there is an experience, and there is in that making I don't know what, call it the paradox, call it the other dimension, but there is an experience of that. Trying to speak it, I think, is how it becomes three-dimensional.*

I understand what you are saying Matthew, because I used to say the same, but what could you make of it other than what you could speak of it?

MATTHEW *I don't know, and that is the weirdness of it, that is the unusualness of it, because normally I can speak very clearly of what I experience. I have found myself in situations during the course of the last couple of weeks talking and then realizing that what I am actually saying is making no sense, and I realize as it's tumbling out of my mouth that it is paradox. Yet I think the place that I am coming from makes absolute sense and is absolutely clear. I could call it absolute truth, but try and speak it, no. I felt very alone and very lost with that, and a little bit idiotic. I often just get a quizzical look, and that is becoming part of the experience, which is very unnerving. Yet it is comforting to realize, ah! There is the paradox again. But as far as communication is concerned it's certainly not the spoken word. It feels like a new game and I am not quite sure how it goes, and yet that is it.*

It's the frustration, I think. I find it frustrating when it's so clear and you can't express it. And I'll try and explain a bit more, very clear to me, difficult to express. I am going to have to choose my words very carefully. There is nothing you can actually make of it more than you can speak of it, because what you speak of it is your limitation of it and what you can't speak about is also your limitation of it. That's why it is all zen, because the understanding I have of an extra dimension emerges as a consequence of my mind reacting to an experience, but the reaction of that experience is always born of my own limitation. There isn't anything the extra dimension can give me outside of my own imagination. There's nothing my mind can make more out of it than its own reaction. There is a belief that it can, a belief widely held across the planet that the mystical experience is outside of any possible knowledge that I could have. This is not true. "I" am what I make of it. Now, that doesn't deny the extra dimension; what it is denying is my ability to express it.

DHYANI *What I see is that even to speak about an extra dimension and the reaction to the experience it creates, or what it can create, is done by the mind. The mind says, "oh there is something I don't have." And that is illusory because it's something everyone is always in or part of, it is nothing outside of one. But when it is said, "I have an experience which I can relate," what then happens is the belief that there is an experience which I don't have but that I could have. This is not possible because it is here all the time, and nobody has ever been out of it or away from it. I can't even say I have an experience because there is nothing "I" can have. I can't even go that far.*

Yes, because there is nothing you can experience outside of yourself. What you have to remember here is we are talking about you and who you are. You are the limit of your own conditioning. The human mind is the product of that conditioning, which is you. To define the experience as being something else would be to define your existence as what I sometimes call a triality – a you, an objective reality outside of you, and everything – and it is not.

What you are both doing now is what I have been doing for years, and that is to try to come to terms with your experience of kensho. And what you are going to have to do is to challenge the resistance that comes from all of your experience secretly desiring something greater than the limit that you now define you are. All of your ambition demands something greater than you are. That is how it works, but in reality you can't do that; you are the limit of your own product.

DHYANI *What I see is that if I create a mystic then I have created a separation, and I see there is none. Therefore I do not have anything that anybody else does not have.*

That's right, and there is always a loathing to admit that because to admit that is to define the limit as simply being you. You are the limit, but you are also everything that exists. To define the experience as something else gives it a credibility that heightens the ambition and need to find some mystical relationship. Once you have acknowledged no separate self exists, that all is an illusion, you are the limit of what you are making. Any ambition is simply a lessening, and whatever might seem to be a credible extension in your experience is in fact a further limitation.

MATTHEW *Is that the inverse nature of the mirror?*

Absolutely, it is working in reverse. You started with everything because that is all that exists. But it has no form or shape; the form or shape is what you make it. To define there is something in between, that there is an additional understanding, is to open the doors to a separate self and get caught within that limitation. That is a place where self will arise again. You are everything and yet nothing. The paradox of that statement encloses the whole of experience, and what you begin to realize is that as the experience expands the demand grows less for you to limit it by demanding something of it.

What is that ever-expanding experience? It is the unspeakable, it is the unsayable, it is the unaskable, it has no substance, shape or form, it just is. It is existence in everything. "I" exist to define that, you exist to define that, and as you define it you create a relative reality of it. I used to believe that reality was something else, that reality was the experience, the everything. But that isn't reality; reality is what I make of everything. That is the only reality there can be unless you define there is a third thing going on somewhere. So everything has no form, no shape, nothing. No thing, but that still isn't reality because reality is what you make it.

What is this experience the mind understands which it can't define? This experience which you can't define is of your making and limitation, and the value lies in you being bold enough to grab that. What you realize is that there lies your limit, because at the end of the day you can't explain 'no thing'. What is happening here is the confusion of mind in expressing things and not making sense of it. You are both trying to express it, like I try to do, and you can't, you only make nonsense. Any definition becomes a zen comment, it becomes a contradiction, because you are trying to make something of nothing.

Let me put it another way, there is everything, nothing. What could it make of itself that you could understand?

MATTHEW *Nothing*.

Then why can't you explain it if it is of your own making? What you have done is you have taken something of that which you have made and then tried to explain that as a further something. In other words, the act of reaction to an extra dimension creates a relationship which you are now trying to explain, but that relationship is of your making, not of its. I used to do this, and if you look at all the mystics they all do it. They all try to substantiate it into some form, an intermediate place, to give it some credibility, some energy, some understanding, and to generate within our own minds some relationship to that.

DEVO *That trying is when they try to talk about it, or as Matthew said when they try to communicate it, to find words for it.*

Which implies that there is something they can't explain, something that does not have a substantial relationship to them. What this is doing is saying my brain is capable of understanding something, or I am capable of understanding something which I can't explain. It is not like that. What can I understand in nothing? How could there be something which I understand but which I can't explain?

DEVO *You may not understand it, but maybe you can like sense it, intuit it?*

But who are you? What has happened is we have gone so far down this road that there is no way out of this because we are in a place now where we cannot give credibility any longer to a mystical relationship. What we can do is give credibility to a mystical experience that we cannot define, but not to a relationship. You should now be starting to be free of the need to make such a relationship. Because if self doesn't exist as a separation then there is no need to make a relationship of separation, although separation is how we exist.

DHYANI *When I was thinking about doing a talk I could see that I was totally struggling, wanting to look at the desires. One was the desire to understand, or basically the desire to get beyond survival. And I saw that no separation can be made in it. Although it's yet another desire it's as if it is cutting survival away, and I could not express it.*

Let me phrase it this way: I am everything that exists, existing as an illusion of separation. This becomes incredibly challenging for someone who still defines themselves as separate because what else is there? What I am beginning to acknowledge is that a reaction of self to an extra dimension is again what I make it, it can't be anything more than that.

DHYANI *And everybody is reacting to an extra dimension all the time.*

Absolutely. But what rightly would we want to make of it? We might want an understanding out of it, how we see it, and then we have limited it to that. I conceptualise it as four dimensions which are an integral part of existence. But if it were separate the mystical experience couldn't exist. As much as that table is part of the room I am part of an extra dimension which is there all the time; it has to be, it never is not. When we acknowledge self as an illusion we begin to unravel the demand to make it anything other than an illusion. Up to that point self was completely separate and therefore an extra dimension would have some substantial benefit to self – just as much as the three dimensions that we live in have. But we are part of a three-dimensional existence. We, you, me, are not part of an extra dimension other than as a totality. That is where the paradox comes in, because as far as "I" am concerned I am separate from it and I fail to see myself as an integral part of that extra dimension.

There is no way of bringing a totality into a relationship, it just doesn't make sense. I haven't got an answer to the question of how the human brain can even notice it, I just don't know. Presumably because it is part of it. I do believe that within another hundred years or so we will have a lot of this taped. We are getting very close now and we are accelerating at enormous rates in terms of our understanding of this. One day mysticism won't be mysticism any more. People will be able to explain the phenomenon of an extra relationship. The fact is, however, that most of the planet, most scientists at the moment don't even believe an extra dimension exists. Whereas scientists are quite prepared to explore the phenomena of five dimensions or multiple-dimensional universes, they don't believe that the human mind can have a relationship to that extra dimension. This is essentially the difference I think between what we're doing here and them. I do think they see that extra dimension as part of existence but they don't believe that the human brain is capable of having a relationship with it. Now mystics do believe it can, and I think this is basically the difference. The mystic claims to have an experience of that extra dimension. Scientists would say there is no way you would be able to know such a dimension, that it is like trying to explain to a two-dimensional man that a third dimension exists, and that it is all born of imagination. .

DEVO *Isn't that what you are saying?*

I am saying it is possible to know that dimension, I'm contradicting science there. It is possible, but it is not possible to make anything of it, to communicate it. The point that could come from this is how does that change you? I don't know, because people tell me I am changing but I am not aware of that. Are you changing Matthew?

MATTHEW *In the acknowledgement of the demand I have of it there is a relaxation, and that is a change. Basically what you have offered me on a practical level is an acknowledgement of my demand of it but from a different perspective, which I would call experience. I would say there is a change because I do feel a bit more relaxed, I don't have to make anything of it.*

Dhyani?

DHYANI *I can't say that I've changed, but it's like as if any demand I placed on it before is falling away and therefore there is no separation with life as it appears. I see that whatever I did before over all the years in order to understand, all the experiences I had, all the satoris, definitely helped me but not to get anywhere close to it. What I see now is that because I have already had the experiences the desire of having anything of it is gone. I could imagine that if somebody suddenly recognizes there is no separate self without ever having had any experiences there could still be a desire for experiences. I can only use a picture for it. It's as if I have a thread and experiences are the pearls I put on it. But it is a separate thing I make and put on the thread, and there is the possibility that if you only see the pearls you don't see the thread. There is a way you can experience the thread. Yet the thread is also irrelevant and the pearl has nothing to do with it either, so anything I experience is only what I limit it to. The limitation is what one can see. But at the same time one can experience no separate self without ever having put any pearl on the thread. Then of course there could still be a desire for a pearl.*

If you experience no separate self inevitably I think you have then got to work out the ramifications of that experience. You can't just leave it, because the experience is there in a permanent state – unlike experiences of satori, which are blinding glimpses of your relationship with it, for I believe that is what a satori is, and they come, they may stay for a while and they go, but there is no permanence there. But with what I am calling kensho the reversal is permanent, the realization doesn't go away. You then have to work with it, to reform everything that surrounds it, because up until that point you have all sorts of understandings about your relationship to life.

Then all the experiences that you have had or believe you have had in your life throw themselves into the cauldron and you need to sort them out. For instance, as a psychic years ago I had absolutely no knowledge of what was happening in a trance because my eyes were tightly shut, yet it would appear that the body was coordinating movements – picking things up from the table, putting things down, and generally moving around, not out of the chair, but with its hands. This has puzzled me many times. Now that I have learnt about what neurologists call 'blind sight' it's really quite possible that all the senses of the brain can be working without the mind, i.e. the thinking process, being aware.

The consequence of the experience of no separate self means I now have to reaffirm my whole relationship with life. To do that seems to take me years, and I am still working with this, as you can gather from what I have been saying. There are still anomalies left which I don't understand, and I don't see it will ever be totally resolved. If somebody, one of you comes along to me and says look, this is how it works, immediately I can see a different relationship is possible. So it is an ongoing thing. It is working out what you have got, working out where you are, and I don't think that it ever stops. It isn't what I make of it. What I make of it is my own reality, and I feel you each could make a different reality out of it.

MATTHEW *And what I understand from what you are saying is that there is no need to make anything of it, and yet you do make something of it.*

Absolutely, because that is what I am, i.e. me David, mind, thought process, brain moving. I am the process of making something of it.

MATTHEW *What has come out of our conversation today is that there is relative reality, and absolute reality does not exist as I exist, does not exist as a three-dimensional experience.*

That is correct. If there is an absolute reality, I don't know it. I have always said that.

By an absolute reality I mean everything. It doesn't have a form or a shape that is you, me. Everything doesn't have solidity, doesn't have liquidity, doesn't have anything of which you are part of. Does an absolute reality exist outside of me as something substantial, as something meaningful as a reality? I honestly don't know, how could "I" know? If we make something of everything does everything have an existence? And if it does how could we know that, how could we ever know that? It isn't that everything doesn't exist – that isn't being questioned. It is whether everything has a reality. You wouldn't say everything is all of the garden, all of the trees, all of us sat here, the greenhouse, the cottage. No, it is not; that is what you have brought it to. That is just another way to create some substantiality for yourself. You can begin to see the wisdom of the old Hindu mystics saying that you create your own reality; you just begin to get a hint of what they mean.

Kensho is the realization that no separate self exists, full stop. That is experiential. Once you don't demand to put something out there to pull in then you have the experience itself of realizing that you do not exist as a separate self.

I don't know what that extra-dimensional relationship is. If it has a totality I can't experience that. I can conceive it has a totality, but experientially it has none other than what you make it. To try and imagine what benefit nothing would have, no-thing would have, challenges the way the mind works. To imagine everything without substance, shape, as nothing, no-thing, has no value whatsoever. So for your ambition there is absolutely no point in having it. But the whole of your survival is dependent on demanding something. How else do you survive without demanding something of everything? All survival, every aspect of what you do, is for self. Then all of a sudden you realize that a separate self is an illusion, but that doesn't mean you don't drink because you are thirsty. It doesn't mean that you don't make love because you want to reproduce. It doesn't mean that all the functions of the human body don't respond in the normal way.

Everything we do is always about self surviving. If I, David, am facing death I will attempt to survive in every way I possibly can, just as much as anyone who hasn't experienced the illusion of a separate self. This is the paradox, that on the one hand you acknowledge you are doing something, on the other hand you experience that you are an illusion. The momentum around the whole thing changes. So I acknowledge that I exist only by turning that everything into something. The paradox becomes almost discernible, not explainable but almost graspable, in the way that you live your life.

Discourses from a retreat

The following five talks are taken from the September 2000 retreat at Sennen in Cornwall attended by ten of David's long-time students.

Tuesday

All of us have spent our entire lives looking for something. Many of you for years have worked with different people, all the time attempting to find something that will have value for you. Yet often you meet somebody who is quite content. I have a friend who is not involved in anything like this. We were schoolmates together and we have always kept in touch. His whole life is about horse racing, county cricket, his family, and it was about his work until he retired. He is totally involved with his life, and it is full. And when you look at this guy he's completely content. It appears he's got everything he needs. Years ago I remember saying to myself, "What's gone wrong with me? Why can't I find contentment by going to cricket, by some activity in the family, and so on?"

I suggest that all of us in this room are like me. Whatever we try just isn't enough, there is something else we need. But that pursuance of something else, it seems to me, is no different than my friend's acceptance. It's simply that he has a level of contentment different to mine. I searched religion, I searched politics, and everything failed, and like you I had a sense of hopelessness. The prison for me was the very environment I lived in. It was like I had a hole in my heart that just couldn't be filled, whatever I tried.

I started this work when I was past forty, and like everything that I do in life I became very obsessive about it. I devoured it, I just couldn't get enough of it, my whole day was spent around it. Then basically through a series of experiences what happened was that suddenly it was like my heart was full. If you look at what I wrote around that period of time you'll see I was claiming I was complete, that I had found it. The problem was I wasn't too sure what it was I had found. Almost as soon as I spoke of feeling complete it wasn't quite right, it always seemed to fall short of it. There was something else. It is only within the last three or four years that I have acknowledged what it was. I hadn't actually achieved completion; I had become free of the need to be complete – and the difference is enormous.

Now the question that arose in our round-the-table discussion last night was whether a commitment can exist to resolve that need, that inner discontent without a motive. I don't believe it can. And that motive can only be survival, for there isn't a single thing we do that doesn't reflect the need of our survival. The paradox then arises that survival itself must therefore create the very motive to be free of itself. It has to be like that or there would be no interest in it for anybody. Somewhere deep within us we acknowledge the inevitability of this challenge. But we can't define it in a way that can give us something to grasp. It's like the walls are just smooth, there's nothing to actually hold onto.

I believe that what I call the hole in the heart syndrome is genetic. I don't think it is a conditioned thing. I think it has its structure in the very origins of our survival itself. For some reason some people have it stronger than others, perhaps just as some people see better than others, some can talk more fluently than others. It is almost as if there is a genetic way of commitment. I'm sure that it manifests itself in a survival demand, because that is all I am. When I'm working with that demand and meet the fear, the anger, the uncertainty, the hopelessness, all such opposition is simply my inability to acknowledge the motive driving my commitment. A motive of commitment exists within me that is beyond simply the survival process, but because I can't make it part of the survival process I easily doubt it's validity.

ROSSANA *Is that the hole in the heart that you are talking about?*

Yes, it's the discontent. Phil last night said it hits him as boredom. It doesn't matter what level of meditation practice you reach you will often hit a level of boredom. You have acknowledged everything, and yet the mind is still trying to resolve something.

Just accept it rather as the motive for your commitment however it manifests itself in you and don't try and resolve it. By doing this you can actually maintain the momentum through what I am calling the hopeless period. The point is to define that commitment simply as it is. It doesn't need to be resolved by survival interpreting it as a motivation to give us nirvana, hope or whatever.

MATTHEW *In my experience, not always but often, the acknowledgment is actually the completion of the circle. It is not important what's being acknowledged, it's not important if motivation is or is not there. The actual acknowledgment lies to rest the disharmony.*

I think that could be the result, but that wouldn't help someone who says that that isn't enough for them.

MATTHEW *But in the acknowledgment they see who they are. That 'who' may not be enough, but I'm not trying to answer it for them, I'm not trying to fill the hole in the heart. The mirror reflects back who you are, not whether it's enough, not whether you feel satisfied. The fact is reflection is happening and in my experience that acknowledgment is the resolution.*

But the question is what makes that enough for you and not for so many others? That is what I'm examining at the moment. Do you see my point, the dilemma that we are facing here?

ROSSANA *Can it be explained?*

No, maybe not. But if someone is sitting in this psychological prison in a state of hopelessness, what's the difference between such a state and what Matthew is saying? The difference has to be in the demand that is being made, and that the desire they have of it is different. The conditioning of others, Matthew, is demanding that there is much more to it than simply what you are giving. They want something else. What makes it okay for you Matthew and not, say, for you Rossana? It has to be the conditioned nature of your desire. That is the only difference.

In your case Matthew what broke that conditioned desire for you?

MATTHEW *The acknowledgment that there is no separation. Somewhere in acknowledging that separation is an illusion the satisfaction occurred, and the ongoing acknowledgment of that illusion has now become the game.*

And for you Phil?

PHIL *I agree with what Matthew said as a psychological process but I think in the end it gets recognized as just that, a psychological process. It's a way of dealing with it as it goes on. It's a way rather of taking a stand, but actually a stand, as far as I can see, is something sitting on top of it all somewhere.*

MATTHEW *For me it is not a stand, it is an experience. It's not a position I have taken to make life appear and feel more acceptable. I know it, it's a reality for me, it's an absolute reality. Not always, not constantly, but more often than not it's a reality. And my motivation and my experience have absolutely altered as a result of that.*

PHIL *Perhaps what bothers me about this is that we are dealing in terms of abstractions and in terms of quite sophisticated concepts, like commitment or whatever. But in actual fact when we look at experience it is nothing but a thought, a sensation, etc. Within that thought and that sensation there is nothing. There are no values as such if you purely just gaze upon them, if you sit there as a witness to them. They are just what they are.*

Let's just hold it a moment. Could we say that what we're talking about here is the value we give to that experience, to that reality, as opposed to its existence?

PHIL *Well I think we are in the realms of value, that is what I am talking about.*

I'm attempting here to express a reflective process. That reflective process is defined by you Matthew as a value, but Phil you are saying it's not that, and then Matthew you are saying it's not that either, each doing it in exactly the opposite way. So coming from both directions is a relationship to that value which is either experiential or a denial of the value of it, whereas in reality they are the same thing.

As you pursue value in it you create a valuelessness. It's hope and hopelessness again. One is a demand for hope, and the other accepts the hopelessness of it. Is there a difference? If you listen to both contributions coming out of the same experience they seem opposite but they are in effect the same thing. In your experience Matthew there is no value. In Phil's experience the relationship to it, the detrimental place to it, is its value. Is there a difference?

PHIL *I'm saying it's making something of something. The mere fact that you are pointing to something as a something in itself is the problem.*

Whereas Matthew is saying the something is quite simply the experience. As I'm seeing it here there isn't really a difference.

Now the question is how do we address what Devo and others are demanding of it? It clearly is a problem because, we will say, they need some substantial motivation to continue.

MATTHEW *But they are the substantial motivation; that is it.*

Has that showed them that it's no longer hopeless?

MATTHEW *But is an answer needed?*

Devo?.

DEVO *It depends what you mean by an answer. In a way no words are needed but still they are. I would say there has to be some resolution. You can say an acceptance, an acknowledgment, an experience, but it is not a matter of words.*

Supposing then we said to you that what is being offered is the freedom from making something of the experience itself. Is that enough commitment?

DEVO *Yes, when it becomes my experience.*

Exactly, can we hold it at that. But what happens in the meantime?

DEVO *In the meantime I look at it. I watch how the hope arises, what I'm looking for to be different, what it is I can't accept, what I want to change. I look at where I am and what I'm dissatisfied with.*

Would that be the power of acknowledgment, Rossana?

Rossana *I think acknowledgment always is, all of the time.*

Isn't that what he is saying? He is not seeking to change it, just seeking to acknowledge it. That is the power of acknowledgment we are talking about; acknowledging something without making something of it, using Phil's words.

Rosemary *Motivation isn't halted by the non-fulfillment of a desire beyond that, which is existence itself almost. Maybe motivation is the wrong word. There is life itself, and the acknowledgment of life itself in each moment is motivation without needing a fulfillment of a desire of it. So there is still going to be desires of something coming on top of that, but there is a motivation that isn't halted by the non-fulfillment of a desire beyond what is.*

Is that enough for you Robert? Is there maybe a resistance to understanding?

Robert *Probably, for if I am illusion then in a way all the rest is just twaddle. It's all thought, it's built on sand.*

Could we say, then, that if it is not illusion it's okay because you have substantiated your identity of survival? The whole of your existence has been dependent on it not being an illusion. So any attempt to understand won't work unless it gives substance to the non-illusive quality of self. Would that be fair?

Robert *Yes, I think so.*

That is the resistance, isn't it? You see it interests me because I remember three or four years ago we had a scientist from America here, and he went through the week and at the end he said to me he was sorry but he hadn't understood a word I'd said. When he went back to his mother and told her what I had said in the talks and discussions, and confessed he didn't understand any of it she said, "Well I do." And it blew him.

So it isn't a question of IQ. It is a question of resistance to acknowledging what is happening within the process of challenge itself. At every level we encounter the nature of our resistance; we simply need to acknowledge that. The power of acknowledgment exists within the experience of the resistance, not in what I say of it. Don't try to understand it. Take hopelessness, take the jail, and acknowledge that that is your attempt to create a substantive quality for self to escape seeing self as an illusion. Just acknowledge what you are doing and see what happens. As the fear approaches there is an acknowledgment, just like Ram Dass with his 'schmoos'. He talks about his 'schmoos' and says out of the corner of his brain it advances, and as he becomes afraid it gains in momentum. He can see the separations there, and it overwhelms him totally. But when he faces it and acknowledges it and sits it down and gives it a glass of water, suddenly he finds that the fear is himself, that it is part of him, that there isn't a separation. That is the experience of non-separation. That thought arising, the movement arising is all "I" am. There is nothing outside of that. But, as Phil says, if we make something of something we have got the separation we want. And that can be not understanding it, being frightened of it, being angry of it, being hopeless of it, resisting it. What we are really resisting is the thought that we are not separate from that process, because our whole survival is built to create the illusion of a separate self.

PHIL *For me witnessing is the faculty, that is what we find ourselves doing, just watching the phenomena. In a sense it is just a stage in the process, a stage most of us are possibly at. But there is nothing else to do, otherwise you are trying to rearrange the world, trying to rearrange the stuff in order for it to fit you. What I call witness is you actually letting it be what it is, whatever that might be. Acknowledge sounds too fancy for me, which is why I baulk at the word. It's like you are actually doing something, whereas I prefer words like witness which are putting it as none of my business really. I'm just watching the show pass by.*

So we have objective awareness, we have acknowledgment, we have witnessing, we have observer – they are essentially all the same thing. There is a witness and a situation being witnessed; there is an observer and an observed situation; there is an acknowledgment by an acknowledger.

ROSSANA *But can't the acknowledger be another separation we can fall into.*

Of course it is, like the witness. But the point is that that is what you are doing, just like you are listening to me. You are a listener, a speaker, that is who you are. Now Robert's dilemma is that that is an illusion. So he's saying what is there? And I'm saying these defence mechanisms are coming up not in an attempt to resolve the situation but in an attempt to protect the separation.

How are we getting on with this?

LYN *I find I have gone tired on this conversation.*

Your way out. Where do you think this escape mechanism comes from Lyn, have you been able to find its origin?

LYN *Can't cope, tired, so withdraw and get away.*

Would it be fair to say that when we can't resolve this we sink into the emotion of it? Would that be true? The unresolvedness of it then sinks into an emotional expression.

Just test every reaction in life. Why do you become angry? Why do you become happy? Why do you become fearful? Isn't the emotion the way out when you can no longer relate to it in a logical way? Anyone who thinks with their emotions, as I've heard many people say to me, is in fact incapable of resolving it and so reverse the process. If we set up a meditation here which was deeply emotional wouldn't that just feed the other way?

The whole struggle is about identity, about separation, and about survival of self. If we were to change the whole momentum of this week and have a great love-in, that would feed all the separation we need and it would be a way out of resolving this. It's simply coming at it from the other direction. So is it fair to argue that there are not two of you, one the intellect and the other the emotional person, but that they are one and the same thing? I have always argued they are, and clearly you are now demonstrating that this is so within your own experience. The inability to resolve it is an emotion. And if we acknowledge that it is, we see that emotion serves almost as a traffic light to show where the relationship of our mind is to life.

Now you might turn around to me and say, are you saying that if I'm happy I have got it wrong? What you have done is reaffirm your identity further than you could possibly have done in any other way. You are strong within the process of happiness, just as you are strong in unhappiness as an emotion. So here is the bit we resolve and here is our way out; we fly off into one direction or another.

ROSEMARY *But also intellectually resolving it is a way out as well, isn't it? It seems the motivation of the brain is to actually resolve things, to work things out. So we move to resolve and identify it; if we can't do that we just flip into the emotions. It is when it is in the middle that it can't be resolved and it can't be unresolved. In a sense that is where it is.*

Okay, but why should being in the middle be right?

ROSEMARY *It is not just that being in the middle is right, because then all you are doing is making another place of it. It is neither being able to resolve it nor not being able to resolve it, and neither is it being in the middle. You can say it is all of it, everything, but again that is making a place of it. You can't limit it to anything.*

So where would acknowledgment be in that?

ROSEMARY *In the motivation of how it is working in both ways; that survival needs to identify itself through resolution or equally through non-resolution.*

Why do we isolate intellectual understanding? Let's go to the motive again. I am saying it is not necessary to separate the three, intellectual, emotional and physical identity. What happens if you do is that identity will jump from one to the other. If "I" can't resolve it, it will escape into an emotional identity. Or if "I" can hold it and think I've solved that one, I'm there now, identity is back again. Or if I hit you on the toe with a hammer you will have a real identity with that. Do we need to separate it? I am trying to show how it is moving because it's been separated by many who see it as two different people, intellectual and emotional, almost as if things can be resolved through emotion or they can be resolved through the intellect or resolved through the physical. Why do we need to divide it? Why can't we just observe what is arising? One is a link to the other, and they all roll into one eventually because their whole purpose is to secure my identity.

PHIL *All you are going to establish really is that every endeavour you make is another attempt to create an identity. Even when people think they are going deep it's actually another mask to wear. It is all endless layers of the onion. We usually have to recognize we are in that process anyway. Whenever you get experiences that you could call transcendental immediately you grab it and say, ah ha, now I'm somebody.*

So the motivation there is identical to the way the thing would slip from one physical or mental state to another. There is no difference really, it is just simply the survival mechanism working in exactly the same way as in every other situation.

RAVEN *Where is the way out in the emotion or in the intellect?*

Who wants to get out?

RAVEN *That is survival I think.*

Yes, but who is that? Is that the body, the mind or you? Do you see? There is no one to get out, is there? The illusion is that you wish to get out, that there is someone to get out. But who is that? It is back again, isn't it? Who is attempting to survive, and you start again. Me, but who is me, who am I?

RAVEN *It's unsolvable.*

Yes it is unresolvable. And the process of acknowledgment is simply to acknowledge that rotation as it is arising. It is almost like an infinite spiral within that understanding. But that acknowledging, that understanding isn't simply a mind movement, it is an experience, the experience that we are talking about.

RAVEN *Yes, but there is still someone who wants to experience.*

Yes, but who is that?

RAVEN *I think that is the trap.*

Agreed, but who is it trapping? You see what we need to do is to be able to catch ourselves as we do this, to be asking a question of ourselves. It's not me being clever with you, that's not what it is about. It is about you being able as you work with yourself to catch the illusion of separation each time.

RAVEN *Always making something of something.*

Yes, that's right. The acknowledgment we are talking about is to be able to hold it at that place, not making anything of it. I am not asking you to change anything, I am simply asking you to acknowledge it. And in the process of that all these problems start to arise, why? Why should there really be a problem in simply acknowledging that we are an illusion? We then can begin to realize that this division, this separation is always seeking a conclusion, always needing to have something external to itself, always wanting to grab something in. It's like it is egotistically motivated towards a possession, or towards an ambition, or towards an identity of a self, a self that doesn't really exist.

RAVEN *But we cannot do anything else can we?*

Exactly. Why should you need to? And there is the freedom.

RAVEN *Freedom is in accepting.*

There is no one to accept. It is an experience. You begin to realize that the very thing that motivates you is the thing that limits you, because you don't exist as a separation.

So let's just summarize this morning a little bit. It has been good because it's really allowing us to focus where it is. I am determined not to let this one slink off into some place where someone will create a value of an identity within this experience because to do so would limit the whole retreat to having some worth for you. If it does have a worth to you then I think it's failed, because it is worth that you came to look for. If you break the boulder and find a lump of gold in the middle then in my opinion your quest has failed. This should really bring you into a place where I am trying to come from with you, as opposed to what you want from this. What comes out then is an acknowledgment of the freedom from needing a lump of gold. That is the ultimate state of human experience for me; maybe there are others but I don't know of them.

Wednesday

All the questions this week have more or less demanded that there should be an objective reality outside of the process itself. Now from my place, whether there is or there isn't is not important. The question is why is that demand so essential in our process. This substantiality can be hope or fear or anger, anything to fulfil the need for a permanent identity. There is nothing wrong in this because that is what you are, and it is no good attempting to change what you are. Nature has designed you to create the illusion of your own substantial reality – called hope, called anger, called fear. That is you. It isn't outside of you, it is you. It has real value in my survival and without it I wouldn't survive. And that hasn't changed in me at all. But it does feel though, as if there has been a change in my brain. This change has created an understanding that out of everything I create something. There is the understanding that that something immediately introduces an opposite. It's almost like that is part of my way of thinking.

If you can just sense this you can begin to see that it can only be the consequence of me not demanding anything outside of what I am making of it. I am not demanding a reality outside of what I create, a reality which can be substantial and from which I can identify a separate place. There is an acknowledgment that from my experience of life I create reality – the glass, the clock, the room, everything, whether physical objects or feelings or intellectual ideas. The belief that there is an objective reality out there creates a substantiality in my identity, external to the illusion of myself. Without that belief it suddenly gets very dark, or it suddenly gets very shapeless.

What then is the experience that is selfless, that has no "I"? How can that experience exist as a realization if I am that process? In other words, Who is there to see? That is a question that has been around me for several years, because I know what I am experiencing. I say I know I am experiencing no self or "I". But it must be "I" that says this otherwise I couldn't tell you about it. There is a contradiction here that is never addressed.

Where am I talking from? Am I talking from my illusion, or can there be an experience that I can have that has no shape or form? And if so how could that possibly happen if the whole basis of "me" is to make shape or form? The question then is can the experience take form as a shapeless, formless, timelessness? Is it possible for me to let go of demanding a shape or a form or a time of my experience? There must be an "I" or a me in it, or I couldn't relate to it; it must be part of my reality. The secret lies in the demand to survive, and if you look at mysticism through the centuries it has always said that.

What creates the anger, the anguish, what creates the experience? I have told you of mine. It was like for months I was hanging onto a cliff and I was afraid to let go, the fear was so great. And then when I did let go nothing happened – except everything. Now, what is that everything I am talking about? Why should that have produced a permanent change in some way, either physically or chemically within my brain, that the whole of my perception has changed? What could have happened? Because this isn't some experience that comes and goes, there is a complete change and I am talking a different language than before. What has produced that? Is it simply conditioning? No, it is not simply conditioning. Rather it is not the demand of form, time or shape out of it. It is acknowledging that every movement I make immediately creates an opposite force. It is acknowledging the process itself, almost like it is a tangible reality within that experience. This comes about only because there isn't a demand for objective reality, there isn't a demand out of fear, or out of anger, or out of hope. And it comes about with the demand of no survival outside of that process. It's almost like you are standing across the duality of your own creation. It's almost like you have blown the myth, blown the illusion.

The problem with the words I'm using is that they will always fall short of what I am trying to say, because they are always bringing it back to a limit which this experience is not. The shapeless, formless, timelessness does not determine an illusion, it does not determine a myth, it does not determine anything. Everything I am doing is the only reality there is of that formlessness. Every word I'm saying here at this moment is a limitation. But we are that limitation.

As I talk I raise more questions than I answer because there isn't a conclusion around this. The conclusion is the process of "I" itself, it isn't where it is going. This is why I am so vehemently opposed to the idea of an objective reality because that will always be a limitation of your perception. Whether an objective reality exists or not is not important for me. What really matters is the motive that motivates you to need an objective reality, not whether such a reality exists or not. You can't ever find it because you are the process of seeking, of finding that reality. But you are not the reality itself, you never can be.

If you stop seeking you are free of the demand to find it, and then you no longer have a tenable interest in survival through that means. So you conclude it's not that, and as you do so you find yourself becoming more and more naked. The only way I can really heighten your own experience of life is to start to challenge what you are making of it by saying it's not that and it's not that, almost in a negative way. It is negative in that it is taking away all the hope of it, all the expectation of it.

The cage you feel yourselves trapped in, hopelessness for instance, is non existent in reality. The cage only exists because you have hope; without hope there is no cage. So the question is how you can be free of hope.

ROBERT *My illusion of living, of being real in a real world is obviously a limitation, but I am necessarily confined to that space.*

You find a resistance because you make the assumption that you are confined to that space. But really you are the process of confining, and there is an incredible difference. Once you have acknowledged that you are the process of confining, what happens, if you accept the nature of opposites, is that in confining "I" can also expand. And the expanding happens at the same time. The problem in expanding is there is no shape or form. Yet paradoxically, the more you limit it the greater the experience becomes. Phil has spoken about bringing it down to a one-pointedness, so the more he sits in meditation and the more he reduces it down to the simplicity of one item, one movement, the greater is his experience of darkness.

That is inevitable, that is how it works, that is the process we are talking about.

Now somehow we have to free our minds of a person being confined, or of a person expanding, and then you begin to get a hint that this is not a concept it is an experience, one that has no boundaries, no limit. It only has a limit if you place an identity of hope on it, or anger, or fear, or anything else you place on it. This is the formless, shapeless, timelessness I am talking about. You can call it God if you like, they are all names meaning the same thing. It has no name, for as soon as you give it a name you define an idea around it, a shape, a form.

PHIL *I would think rather in terms of negation; it is a negation of all experience, of all function.*

In other words it's not that, it's not that, it's not that. Whereas at the moment half of us are saying it is that, it is that, it is that. But as we are doing this we are also creating it's not that, it's not that. We have to be free of the idea that there is someone either negating or affirming, and just see it as a process. Once we acknowledge that we are simply a process we have lost the need to identify ourselves within that process. And then there is an experience that I can have of nothing, of darkness, of shapelessness, of existence.

The possessive, ambitious nature of ego, however, will always substantiate its identity, that there is still someone to do this or to do that, because it needs to do so for you to survive. So you meet the paradox here where really nothing in the way you behave changes but everything is different, and as that difference moves, and it's always in movement, you have got a lifetime's work ahead of you. Kensho isn't the finish of the day, it's the beginning. You have to start all over again from an entirely different relationship.

In every movement of this process of survival there will always be a need to identify form and shape, which will be done in accordance with our conditioning. There will always be a need to demand a conclusion, a possession of experience. Imagination will always attempt to create a place out of experience where it would like to be.

And ego is the structure of this process. We are free to let that happen if we don't give substance to a demand, a place, or object of "I" or me existing within it, but just acknowledge ego as the movement itself.

This is what meditation is, just letting things fall away from what is happening. Yes, I will always attempt to identify myself; yes, I will always attempt to possess something for myself; yes, I will always have ambition for myself. But if myself is simply the process of survival, I can let it go at that. I don't have to stand in some rigidity that is frightened, that judges, that demands. I can see the whole perfection of what is happening.

Kensho is the realization of that perfection and movement, the realization that there is no one to hang onto anything. At this point a change begins. Not in the demands of your ambition, your possessiveness, or your identity, because these are your conditioning, but you are free of demanding anything more. You are truly working with the experience as it arises, which will always be your conditioned limit.

The paradox of the whole experience is that you come to this incredible position where you really don't feel any different, you are what you are, and at the same time somehow that is perfect. Suddenly the hole that was there before, the demand, the inadequacy has gone. You are free of any such demand because you don't need to identify with it anymore, you don't need to be ambitious of it or possessive of it.

Motivation is the key here, because now there is nothing left to motivate us but we are still being motivated. This motivation is not something that is a result of our conditioning but has its origins at the time of our birth, even in creation itself. It is how evolution, the development of existence takes place. The brain is existence experiencing itself, and it couldn't do that if it didn't have this genetic need for "I". Through the illusion of separation existence knows itself. There may be another way, but to me it is quite perfect. It only seems complicated because it is paradoxical, otherwise it is very simple.

There is really no separation between everything and your experience. We are forced into a place of intellectualizing the purpose of our species because we see our own species as being separate from everything. The mystic does not see our species in this way. He or she sees it simply as a manifestation of the totality. But the beauty of creating a separation is that you do create an intellectual understanding. To intellectualize is not a waste but is an essential ingredient in the whole process, because intellect can change reality. You create your reality, yet that reality is also existence's reality, there is no difference. So existence can sit back in you and intellectualize hypotheses that can become an extension of reality.

Kensho throws up a completely different relationship to your experience. You have always assumed that you were separate from the process of existence to intellectualize, or to feel, and that somewhere there was a perfect place of your own conditioned demand. But kensho is saying that because you are an illusion it is existence's experience, not yours. The ramifications of this are enormous and what they do in my mind is overawe me with the magnificence of it all. I don't need anything else.

If you are looking for carrots, there are bundles of carrots. I don't know about you but if I was looking at it from a separate point of view I would trade that any day for any hope, any fear, any anger. To me those are very limited relationships. Sat in this room now existence is attempting to resolve itself. Can't you sense the beauty of this whole process?

An experience of the realization that "I" am not separate, that "I" is an illusion, is only possible if you don't demand a resolution of that experience by making a definition of it, such as objective reality, or hope. To me it is fluid, it needs no place, it is in constant movement. I am part of that as much as you are, no more, no less, just part of it, free to move with that experience. Then you see the beauty of the mother with her child fighting for its survival. You see survival working in the struggle of relationships, you see it in people fighting for their lives in sickness. You see the whole thing in its totality for you have lost the need to pull out something from this totality other than your own need to survive.

I still have that survival need, so if I have a headache I take an aspirin. I don't have a problem with that, it's part of the perfection of the whole thing. I don't have to meditate in a certain way, I don't have to define what's right and wrong in the order of things. Everything I do creates a limitation of it, but I acknowledge that that limitation is part of the perfection of life itself, is how life works.

Now can you see what is on offer here, not to you but to the universe, because the fact that you need this must be the universe's demand of it, otherwise you wouldn't seek it. Nothing that is happening is a mistake or wrong. The frustration that we all experience isn't a wrong view of it, it is part of the universe's struggle. And the inability to catch that moment is also perfect, it's also how it works.

So I see our work as constantly trying to loosen up the identity within this experience. The more you focus it down in your meditation practice you find out what it isn't, and what Phil, like Eckhart, called the darkness grows greater. There isn't a fear of that darkness; that darkness isn't substantial or identified in terms of existence, or formlessness, or timelessness. It is a reality beyond identification, a reality beyond ambition, a reality beyond timelessness. And if it exists as an absolute I can't have it because I am its process of making it into something. So every statement I am making, everything you are sharing with me this morning, is by its nature a limitation. But that is its reality too.

In letting go of your own limitations, every moment of the day there is change, but it is lost immediately because there is still something demanded of it – a hope, a fear. So our work is letting go, taking out the restrictions that would make it something, and thereby opening the experience to where it really is. The need, the hope, the hole, whatever you want to call it, is part of the illusion; it doesn't really exist at all. So when I let go of the cliff nothing happened; why should it? Where had I got to go?

Then you realize intellectually the role of *homo sapiens* as a species. It has taken over the entire planet and more importantly it is now determining what that planet should be. But supposing I am right and separation is an illusion then it is the planet determining itself. Survival is the motivation by which this happens. In every movement of *homo sapiens* survival can be seen, and if it weren't there it wouldn't work.

Thursday

We have to generate within ourselves the self-reflection to be able to see exactly what is happening. When we are talking to somebody, for instance, about some aspect of our lives, apprehension might start to arise within us concerning our identity. It may be fear, it may be feeling a victim, it may be anger. We then feel a need to redefine our idea of a *status quo*, a certitude within ourselves. It is not a question of what you are saying or doing but of your need to identify a positivity within any situation in accordance with your own conditioning. This same need appears in everything you do.

Everywhere I meet people doing this, criticizing, judging, always establishing some identity for themselves. It isn't wrong, it's perfect, it is how they survive by projecting their own theological, spiritual, moral relationships into what they find in life. But do they understand, do they acknowledge what they are doing? Do they truly know themselves? In breaking up that need for solidity, what you begin to realize is that it doesn't need to change, it just needs to be acknowledged, to be recognized. Then you can understand its perfection in motivating you.

The key to what I am talking about here is that sufferer, feeler, thinker, are all the same thing, they are all based on a need for a separate identity. Kensho lets you experience that there is no judger, there is no feeler, there is no thinker, there is no sufferer, that the process of brain is all there is.

Such an understanding makes you realize you are responsible for your own suffering. Now you notice I haven't said pain. Pain comes and goes, we all have pain. But suffering is of our manufacture; it is the demand that we place on pain. Suffering is the consequence of some desire held, you will never find it is not. And if I can simply acknowledge the perfection of suffering I don't have to be the victim of it. You don't have to swing each side of your demands of suffering. Suffering is part of life, it is part of experience.

At whatever level you are working with this it works the same, whether it is about death, whether it is about how you wish your relationship with your loved ones should be. This is the stuff of life, and if we can truly acknowledge what is happening as it is presented to us in these challenges, as opposed to what we want to happen, there is a whole different place. If I am frightened, I acknowledge that I'm frightened and I immediately acknowledge the value of that fear. And once I have acknowledged its value its intensity diminishes. It only increased in intensity because I didn't want it. The same applies to anger and to everything else. It is a different relationship altogether.

In the freedom of this experience there is a carrot. So although I have presented this work so far as being completely hopeless, completely bottomless, with nothing to offer, I am now also saying that an acknowledgment of what you are changes your relationship with life. But it will not meet your desires. There is indeed a big juicy carrot – once you are free from demanding one. That is the paradox.

The illusion of "I" is always apparent in the moment of now and in everything you do. If you stop running off into the thinker or the feeler you will see a much bigger picture, because as you narrow it down to a point, the darkness, the formlessness gets greater. I say it is the ultimate human experience because it deals with the ultimate value of our existence in life. This ultimate human experience has no limit, has no place, has no purpose, and has no method. It encompasses all places, all purposes, and all methods. It encompasses it all.

ROBERT *Is the mind all that exists?*

Rather all that exists is what the mind makes of it. You don't exist, because the mind doesn't exist. To my brain that is real.

ROBERT *So feelings are just a function of the mind?*

Of the brain. I have to say that Robert, because I don't know where your mind is. I know where your brain is, and that is what starts working when you have a feeling. Brain is much more substantial than your mind, you can look on a body scan and see it. You can't do that with your mind. I can measure the neurological movements of your brain; I don't know where your mind is. For me brain is real, mind is not. But my brain wouldn't be real without my mind, without the illusion of my mind.

ROBERT *Taking a slightly different angle I was thinking about death and what occurred to me is I have never been dead and I never will be dead. I will always be alive.*

For me, you have never been born, only brain has. When brain dies the illusion of "I" ceases. Brain is the determining factor in my existence. When brain lights up consciousness can exist; when brain doesn't light up consciousness cannot exist, and consciousness is me. What we can't find is you other than as consciousness.

What is at stake here is your demand for separation, your need to give substance to your own identity as separate from everything else. That separate identity has taken fifteen-thousand million years to evolve, it is not going to let go easily.

ROBERT *Aren't you also substantiating your identity?*

Indeed I am, but from the point of view of acknowledging that identity is an illusion. You are not prepared to accept that. At some point, because I have taken that resistance away, it became an experience for me.

DEVO *When you said feelings are just a function of brain, for me there is a difference between thinking based upon feeling and what I would call purely intellectual thinking.*

What you are doing is you are grading thoughts in accordance with your need to survive. In other words there are two me's, but really they are the same thing. There isn't any difference because the next thing you will do is divide something else up inside, so you can slip off into somewhere else. There is only one process here.

Take the example of objective reality. Robert has tried to establish that there is such a thing as an objective reality. I say the reason he needs to do that is because he needs to substantiate an identity for himself that is real too. As long as he could hold onto such a belief he didn't have to confront his own illusion.

Now aren't you doing the same? Aren't you saying you can let this piece go because you can hang onto this other one? There is only one you, and that you is an illusion. Your relationship in terms of feeling, intellectual thought, judging is all one thing. You feel one illusion, and there are various things you can do as that illusion. What you can't do, it seems, is to challenge your identity, for that is a very different and frightening thing. Judgment is an attempt to affirm identity. Fear, anger, all emotions are an attempt to reaffirm identity, just like thought is. They are all the same.

I am not looking to solve the illusion, not looking as a scientist does to gain a complete understanding of the brain. The same motivation that allows somebody to do a dynamic meditation of jumping up and down is the same thing that makes you sit and read a book. There is no difference. The feeling that comes out of that dynamic meditation substantiates an identity; part of your identity is getting it right, being academically clever. So society complements identity when it calls you a doctor, a professor, or even a guru, and what it's doing is giving identity and separation through status and importance.

From the simplest finger movement to the deepest, profoundest feeling it is all a process of maintaining a sense of a separate identity. It is so simple, but mind can't allow it to be that simple, because to do so denies your own importance. If kensho can be difficult then we can feel important. Look at the different teachers and gurus, ego is coming out of their ears.

MATTHEW *I guess what I find a little bit murky in this conversation is the process of you using words to show self the illusion of self, and then the representation of self in the form of words or argument. What I miss in myself is that mirroring to recognize it exactly as it is happening because I get distracted by the argument. My frustration isn't the words; my frustra-*

tion is my inability to reflect what is actually happening in terms of the self. Where I go is my desire to have an identity in understanding what is being said, rather than actually recognizing the utter beauty in what is happening. That is my frustration.

Isn't that understandable because all your life you have listened to and tried to respond to another's point of view. Whereas what we are doing this week is to see a conversation as an example of how self is creating an identity out of the very conversation, to see the way the mind is all the time trying to create a relationship with itself. What I am saying is that whatever arises in our discussion is an attempt to create identity.

In Zen it is called words to overcome words. Yes, I can accept your frustration, but what I am seeing here is quite magnificent because it is a constant attempt to construct a dimensional reality called self. We put it into a very hallowed space here because we are caught within each other's relationship to our work. But wherever you go, when you walk down the street, when you walk into a shop, whatever your activities are, you will see exactly the same thing working.

Part of you will acknowledge the perfection of that separate self. You begin to understand its beauty and its magnificence in terms of how that illusion can solidify itself into a reality, a reality which allows that separation to exist as a separate person walking about. It is just absolutely fantastic. Blows my mind. So whereas you are trying to resolve that place, I am admiring the beauty of it.

MATTHEW *How do we support the polishing of the mirror?*

Out of your experience in the movement of life. Do I get frustrated, angry, fearful? Yes, of course I do. But what I would have done before would have been to attempt to resolve that anger, that fear, that frustration. Now I tend to see the perfection of it, to see its magnificence. It leads to a deeper balance, because doing so is observing it as it is arising as opposed to trying to reach a conclusion. It is so perfect. It is nature's way of protecting me as an illusion. It is a very beautiful thing.

If I stand in the frustration, if I stand in the anger, if I stand in the fear, I am what the movement of life intends me to be. So if someone makes me angry do I respond to that anger? Yes I do. Do I respond differently than I would have done in the past? Probably. In the past I would most likely have punched them, now I tend to try to reason with them. So I am a little bit better if you like.

DEVO *Is there still the illusion of a you or an I?*

Yes, as an acknowledgment of its illusion. The duality is as it is. I would venture to suggest the sole difference between us is I can live in acknowledgment of my duality, you have a need to resolve it. That is the only difference at this moment in time. Robert put it very well when he said if I stand on one foot I know it is an illusion, if I stand on the other foot I experience a reality of separation. The difference is I accept the paradox of life working. What's the problem? Why it is a problem is the separation you are making of it.

The simplicity of this should now be realized. It is not difficult. It isn't about resolving emotions or resolving intellect, it is about experiencing the value of the illusion of separation and observing it. The famous saying of Buddha is very evident for me: he who truly knows himself is master of the universe. It's about that, it really is. I am not pretending for one moment I am a master of the universe; that is a lifetime's work. But there is a simple relationship to the illusion of separation, which is completely opposite to the way the mind, would work. So there are two things going on here; an acknowledgment of the perfection of what is arising, and asking what is motivating me to seek a resolution. That is it. Then immediately you will be drawn back to the question of the identity of "I". Always look for your need to give substance to an identity. And to do that requires patience. We play games intellectually, or we play games emotionally, but really identity is the key.

When realization, when kensho is your experience you will almost kick yourself. You will say is that all there is? It is so simple, it is as clear as my hand in front of my face, but it is obstructed by the motives of what you make of it. I don't need to resolve the paradox. I don't need to resolve duality; duality simply is.

Friday

I would like to begin this morning by looking at our work from the aspect of choice. If "I" am not an illusion then choice is real, but if the sense of a separate "I" is an illusion then choice is determined solely by the brain in terms of its survival. Realizing this puts a different connotation altogether onto the reality of choice, onto its function, its truth.

As you make choices you have in your mind an idea of what is the truthful choice to make, what is the correct choice to make and by reaffirming that choice as a truth you are again creating an identity of your own separation and reaffirming your own survival. But, as I've said many times, truth is never absolute; it is always relative, a truth that I make to complement my own survival. I am reaffirming the illusion of "I" as my personal experience, but that doesn't make it true. That is simply a choice you are given in terms of your own identity.

DEVO *It's true for you.*

It is what I do. I don't actually see it as true for me because I see it as part of the reaffirmation of my identity.

ROSEMARY *Otherwise you create some absolute truth again, and fall into the same trap.*

I am speaking to you out of my experience, but you may say that is only my truth and I would have to agree, for it is a truth I have made from separation. My choice may well change, and as it changes my identity changes. But this process is necessary so that I can identify the illusion that is me. This is why out of kensho nothing really changes, because what is happening is essential for survival. If it didn't work like that I couldn't survive. If I suddenly decided one day that because I am an illusion there is no choice then I would no longer function.

So how can I function if I am an illusion? Well the fact is I do, and that's it; there is the paradox. Realize that as you affirm choice you are affirming your identity; it isn't right, it isn't wrong, it is what you do. This is what is realized in what I call the experience of kensho.

The whole process of identity is that it is how nature is able to define a reality through us. Nature can't define a reality unless we as separators define it for nature. We can call it God's choice if you like or life's choice, they are all the same to me. So looking at the zen of it, everything that you make of nature, of life is nature's choice because you are not separate from nature. You can see the whole beauty of God, or Nature, or Life, or whatever you want to call it, working in its own self-reflection. It's brilliant.

Why nature needs to know itself I don't know, but once you accept that "I" am an illusion that is what's happening. Hence the wisdom of the old Zen masters saying if God exists, He doesn't. If Life exists, it doesn't. If the cup is there, it's not. You can begin to sense the incredible insight of those old Zen masters, just begin to see the self reflection of Seng-ts'an. What is really going on is far broader than the limitations the demands of our minds make of it. What is happening is absolutely unbelievable. Through the simple illusion of separation an entire universe knows itself.

ROBERT *When you say the entire universe knows itself, surely it can know itself only as a limitation?*

In kensho, brain makes no identity of separation. It is "I" that makes the identity of separation to bring everything into something. Now is it possible for the universe to know everything? If you want my opinion as a limitation I think it does, otherwise I don't think kensho would be possible. When the brain is open to everything, as J. Krishnamurti said it could be, the universe is open to everything, for there is no division. But the only way brain can make something of everything is in the limitation you make. Now why that is needed don't ask me; how can I know that since "I" am its process not its conclusion. So if God exists, it exists in its totality as everything, without a separate identity. I am not in a position of knowing anything more than that, so why hazard a guess? But I am in a position of experiencing brain open to everything. The problem is this has no value until I make something of it, and that something is all "I" am.

The awareness of the universe as far as either you or I are concerned is the ability to create a limitation within life. That limitation gives each of us an identity, and as each of us creates an identity this gives objects an identity. So when we go back to vipassana we can see that sense object, sense base is really how the universe knows itself.

Once you realize that everything you do in life is about determining your own identity there is an experience waiting there that allows you to be free of the need to demand an absolute out of that realization. Such a demand isn't needed, you are free of it, you understand the beauty of the mechanism itself. Kensho comes as almost an overwhelming appreciation of the whole process, and the value of kensho is in this freedom. It doesn't have to define itself within the narrow limits of your choice.

Devo *Is the experience itself a limitation?*

No, the experience is of itself. Life, Nature, God, Existence, I don't mind what you call it because it's all the same thing, has no limit, no division, no separation. What you make of it is your limitation. Once you understand this you recognize there is no way for you to beat the process, and you are free from the need to beat it.

Rosemary *There is no solidity of a place for "I" to go to, to hide in.*

Exactly, there is no solidity for you to go to. You are the process of making it solid because that is what you are, and you can never make anything more of it than that. What's the problem? The problem is that that is not what "I" wants.

My role as I see it is helping you to polish your mirror. But you see your role as polishing the mirror in order to see in it your own ambition of life, and there is a vast difference. The purpose of cleaning your mirror is so you can become more objectively aware of your own limitations. The practice of our work is very much about this. I might suggest you sit for a minimum of half an hour, do a walking meditation, do whatever else you do mindfully, and that that will clear the mirror. It does, and then you come back and say you are even more frustrated than before because now you can clearly see what you want, you get a true reflection, and find you can no longer fulfil your ambition. The role of the discourse in the mornings is to challenge what you would like to see in the mirror when you look whilst at the same time, hopefully, not putting anything else in it's place.

When I talk of freedom I am talking of the freedom to look in your mirror and see what is there. I am not talking of freedom as a demand that you want out of polishing the mirror. But most people clean the mirror with a view to see in it what they want. So there has to be a two way process here, one to clean it and the other to challenge your expectations of what you want to see in the mirror. There is a completely different understanding you can move into that is far, far bigger, and this is the freedom not to identify with any limitation.

As I raise your own need for identification in an intense way and bring it sharply to focus I am saying you have within you all the seeds you need of this plant, this freedom. It exists within you; unlock it not by changing it but simply by acknowledging what is happening. Then suddenly you say who cares, for you can see the whole beauty. You may still care passionately because caring passionately is who you are. But you understand that, and understanding it means you do not have to affirm a truth, a right or wrong in any fundamentalist way.

ROBERT *Can you get into a position of not caring passionately?*

Yes, there is a real risk of that, but doing that is just the opposite. In a sense it isn't all the same because it is nature defining it. It is right that you should affirm one or the other choice, but recognize that by doing so you are creating an identity.

So the central key always is that identification is what motivates choice, and choice is the key manifestation of survival. Possessiveness and ambition complement that central core of ego, of you. I can no longer find any way to separate ego from myself. I know I am the process of ego, there isn't someone to separate it out; ego is my identity.

DEVO *But isn't there a certain dis-identification?*

Yes.

DEVO *So you are both an identity and yet you are not an identity.*

When you see a cup, within your own process you see it as separate from you. In reality that is not true. The forming of a separate thought of it creates the identity that is you. If you demand of life that all you see is a cup, a tree, what you call the real world, then you are going to limit everything to what you make out of it. And that is not what it is all about, you will miss the whole ambience of the experience. When you cease seeking to place your own identity in the object, what is called objective awareness, then what happens is the experience starts to come to you. But any reaction you make will always create a limitation. You might walk around the corner and look at the view and there would be a moment when you weren't separate from everything, and you might say "wow". Doing so immediately puts you back into your separation, your limitations – that it is a beautiful view, an ugly view, a hideous view. Whatever you name it is what you limit it down to. The experience is that at the point the cup or the view ceases there is nothing to be seen – but everything, in which there is nothing!

The experience of seeing the cup separately is no different to the experience of seeing the ego separately; it is exactly the same. All activity in terms of self-identity comes out of that single experience. There isn't a situation where you work through cup, identity, possessiveness, ambition. Everything comes back to the something you make it. You are the process of making it something, you are not separate from that process. But what does happen is that suddenly you realize that you are the process that makes the cup just as you are the process that makes the ego. And you realize there is no difference between either process. I know it is a paradox, because who is making cup or ego? The process is of itself.

Now you find it easy to understand that if I don't see the cup I can see the table, and if I don't limit it to the table I can see the room. You can understand that, but when it comes to your own emotions, your own demands you won't do that. It is no different whether I limit myself to universal love or I limit myself to a cup. There is no difference; one is simply a psychological process, the other is a physical process, but they are absolutely the same process.

Am I big enough to take that quantum leap and for the first time stand right outside in an understanding of all the limitations I make? I don't have to affirm my identity in these narrow limits, and they are narrow limits even in the way we form the world or how we see God. The ultimate human challenge is to stand outside of all your limitations. This is scary because it is starting to dismantle your identity structure. The strange thing is you don't lose anything because at the end of the day you come to realize the value of having those limitations. But you are no longer a prisoner of them, you have moved outside your own shackles.

Saturday

I have been asked to place my own experience in relation to what we have been discussing this week. The danger of doing this is that it can create a framework of desire around it, and one has to be very cautious about that.

My role here is to build an opportunity for self-reflection, to be a mirror. The key is commitment, it is how badly you want it. The people who seem to achieve the greatest movement of self-reflection within themselves are the people who work the hardest. There is not an easy ride on this, I really don't believe there is. The momentum is up to you. And there are escape routes but they are temporary whatever their form – social engagements, ideas, a hobby, maybe even drugs. They don't resolve anything and at their conclusion you are back where you started from, in some cases often worse off. What we are doing here is turning off every avenue of escape.

Some of you have said you feel hopeless, but there is a hope in this for there is a point of no return to that hopelessness. There is the freedom to make that hope the key. And if a desire is there it is a desire out of the dilemma of wanting something from it. At first I was confused by my own experience because I had this sense of completion and so I was claiming an identity of being complete. But as I applied the illusion of self to what I had experienced a totally different relationship became apparent, one where I was free of the need to be complete. To me that freedom is the ultimate experience.

As we bring the "I" into ever-sharper contrast you have to face the fact that your whole life is around the protection of the illusion of the solidity of "I". As you slow down through meditation the whole movement of "I", you heighten the contradiction. You create a solidity of "I", the very opposite to what you believe you are doing. "I" seems solid almost, yet it also seems less, and as that happens the space around it becomes incredibly terrifying. It becomes terrifying because it is as if it has got nothing to catch hold of. It is exposed in its own insecurity, in its own fear, terror, anger, whatever you like to call it, which is a reaction to what is happening around you, a reaction to the expansion of the darkness, as Phil calls it. A timeless, shapeless, formlessness is what I call it. Matthew uses Osho's term and speaks of existence. The name doesn't matter, it is only what we have limited it to. There isn't a Truth. It is simply "I" limiting the illusion down to a place where self can be terrified. "I" can be frightened because it is almost an unnatural state. Historically you hear of people breaking out into a sweat and you hear experiences of incredible uncomfortableness at this level. Then there is a point where the "I" starts to dissolve. And as "I" dissolves, panic increases and immediately you pull "I" back again. Speaking personally, this will happen many times with this experience.

At some point it is as if the dissolving of "I" is witnessed by itself, giving up almost its demand for separation, and at the final point of that formlessness, shapelessness, darkness, existence, is a real experience of the remnant left of "I" – and then there is nothing. That nothing can be a microsecond long or a thousand years long, you don't know. The whole recognition process has ceased. However long is not important for it is timeless and you have no knowledge of it whatsoever. And at that moment of contact, taking my old analogy of the pen on the paper, as the "I" re-forms you experience again, through the process of the illusion of the separation of "I", a timeless, shapeless formlessness, a darkness, whatever you are going to call it. As the "I" re-forms after that experience you catch it, like it comes back. You have witnessed yourself ceasing to exist and re-emerging, and out of that re-emergence you witness momentarily a timeless, shapeless, formlessness.

Out of that place you re-establish an illusion, and you find that you are really no different than you were before. Why should you be? Everything that is working works the same, but it is like it has come from the opposite way, and there is a quality in your perception that has changed permanently. It isn't a temporary phenomenon, it doesn't go, it is permanent. In everything that I see there now seems to be a deeper dimensional relationship which I didn't notice before. It isn't something I can have substantially, it has no value to me. It has nothing I can take from it. So if I look at that candlestick it's like there is a depth to it that wasn't there before, there is a quality about it that has changed. Something in the brain has changed, something has altered, which is giving me a totally altered perspective than I had before, but, and I keep saying this, there is no value in it. The only value, if you must have one, lies in my attitude to life, because the need to be complete has disappeared.

I believe there was just a moment in that experience, which to an extent is still evident within me, where just before I lost it I almost became aware of the brain experiencing itself. But I can't be sure of that. The illusion that is you is brain experiencing itself, nothing else, and for a moment it was like that illusion disappeared. I can't make anything of it because I am dependent on the making something of it. But there was just that moment, I don't know how long or how short it was. I am calling it a moment because that is all I can make of it. That moment could be fifteen-thousand million years, it could be a second. It doesn't have a time base at all, hence you get the mystic talk about the totality of timeless experience.

There is nothing magical about this, it is just using what you have and the commitment and patience to work with what you carry with you in terms of yourself. The reason I am telling you this is because it is a simple, practical, self-experiencing thing. It doesn't have a mystical content for me anymore, and even the word mystic I guess at this point has to be challenged. There isn't something out there, and if there is I don't know about it, I am simply its expression. But what this freedom has done is to give me a faith in life which I didn't have before. It has given me the ability of looking at things from the point of their perfection and not from my expectation of them. My expectation of them is there, that hasn't ceased, but that is all about my survival. I can look at the paradoxical nature of each situation arising. I can sense it in the movement of everything, and realize so to speak, as Robert has said, that there are two feet, the foot that says I need to survive and the foot of the illusion that says it is a paradox.

We can't work out why we have to be an illusion, other than that the brain needs a self-reflection. I have let go of all need to understand, so there isn't a need for any religious concepts surrounding it, soul, rebirth, karma, there isn't a need for a philosophical idea of mysticism. Suddenly the beauty, the magnificence of the now emerges. Colours increase in intensity because I don't want them any different. Relationships have different meanings that run to great depths of understanding. The whole perspective has changed because I am not demanding anything of it. The feelings are there, the terror, the fear, the anger, the boredom, the relief, and they are acknowledged within the paradoxical movement of things for the value they have to me in my survival. There is a whole different place that wasn't evident before, not in terms of self-discovery, hope, or anything else, but in the perfection of its own existence.

That was my experience, and now I have to work with that to try and make sense of what is happening. I need to do that in my life, I can't just sit there and be calm and say it's nothingness and shapelessness. I can't do that, it's not in my character. I don't know why but it is uniquely me to have to work with it.

You can objectify very clearly someone else's movement but it is difficult to acknowledge your own and to see yourself. That is why the mirror is essential to throw back a self-reflection. The slowing down in the meditations and the silence has been the place where that has been able to happen, without the constant interference of our everyday lives. This is an important process in self-discovery because it is something you can walk with wherever you are, it isn't just valid in one part of your life, it is there all the time, and there isn't one place that is better than another.

An analogy would be when you started to ride a bicycle. At first you had to get on the bicycle with your parents or somebody holding the bicycle for the first few pedals until you learnt to balance. And then after you have learnt how, it becomes so natural that you don't even think about it any more. That's the situation I want you to commit yourselves to in terms of your own self-reflection in every day of your life. If you work with that it will happen.

Don't hold my experience as a norm or a datum. It is where I find myself, and it is not the end of the road. I have as long as I live, a lifetime's work with that. As I go along I change my mind, and what I have given you this morning is a limitation, it can never be anything else because it is who I am. And as you judge that limitation, you judge it as right or wrong by your own limitation. That is part of the perfection, that is part of the process.

This process seems a very serious business for it challenges all the emotional states, all ideas of love. It challenges the intellect too at every level. The process is in itself, it isn't what you make of it. The journey is more important than the goal, because the journey is what we are. The goal is just some idea we have thought up or that we have got from someone else. The journey is living in the now. This is what the mystic means by the now, he doesn't mean it is going to lead to something. If he does then he is caught within his or her own ambition of it.

I haven't got it all right. And I have to be big enough to say it isn't as it was, it is changing all the time for me. It has taken me nearly four years to actually give you this conclusion this morning, and even that isn't right. It's going to take me the rest of my life and it still won't be right, it will still be what I am making of it. But the goal was about being free and I am free. I am free to die, I am free to suffer, I am free to be angry, I am free to be terrified. Then suddenly, as Ram Dass says, it is not so important any more. What do I now need to claim other than the experience itself? Where do I need to go other than where I am? What's the big deal I'm making of this? You can see now the simplicity of standing in that experience.

So the desire to take a walk to the nearby village of Sennen is the desire held that separates me in the course of that walk from the experience of the walk itself. And as I am walking along I am realizing that the experience of the walk is far more important than going to Sennen. I am free of the demand to be there. But I acknowledge the paradox of the desire, and I acknowledge the value in my perfection and desire of survival in wanting to get there. Replace Sennen by the need for freedom and you see that freedom isn't something you can have, it is something you experience. It isn't any conceptual relationship whatsoever to anything you can imagine. It is, and it stands within its own place and its own experience. If you can sense that you have got your own opportunity to work towards your own freedom.

There is indeed such a thing as commitment without motive. See the value of your own experience and build on that. Just don't see my rhetoric as being important. I am just a means by which to work beyond it. And beyond it is a recognition of your own experience and your own relationship to it. Use your own experience as a base from which to work. That is your guru, not what I have said this morning. I have just told you a whole load of stuff it isn't.

zen

Extracts from a talk given in Austria, 2000

The most important question for me is, "What is zen?" Such a question is an ultimate question. The ultimate question of mind is, "Who is I?" But to ask what is zen is the ultimate question of life.

Zen arose in China, where it is called Ch'an, and emerged in strength around the 12th and 13th centuries in Japan, where it became Zen. The early Zen patriarchs, as they are called, were clearly men who had a different vision. They brought together Taoism and Buddhism and what emerged was Zen Buddhism. But this is not what I mean by zen. I am not a Zen Buddhist, and the zen we are talking about didn't have an allegiance to Buddhism itself but more to the Masters themselves. Today in the world there is more zen practised outside Japan than there is in it, because this zen is not about an idea or a method.

It can easily get confused in the West with mysticism, because mysticism is understood, for example, as seeing the universe in a grain of sand; but that really is pantheism. Pantheism is a limit, and zen knows no limits. This zen I am talking about is simply a word relating to the ultimate experience of life. Wherever you walk and from whatever path you come zen is always with you, because zen faces the paradox; zen is the paradox, zen is no paradox.

Zen refers to an experience rather than to an idea. It is indescribable, but to be able to approach a relationship with it we use words in order to transcend words, and we use intellect in order to transcend the intellect. Often when the work gets to a very sharp place we adopt a different relationship. We might use jokes, we might use violence, we might use poetry, we might use music, we might use art.

Take the art of Picasso. I used to look at Cubism and say it was a load of rubbish, women with breasts facing the wrong way, and it really didn't make any sense. But yes it does, for the Cubist vision is an experience, not something that is a logical, intellectual thing. But that does not mean I sink into sympathy or emotion about Cubism. Nor do I listen to poetry and feel all emotional. With music it can be the same. A certain sequence of notes may take us into a different relationship, but again this is not an emotional experience.

Zen is the sum greater than the state of opposites. Opposites are what we limit it to when we are reacting with our minds. If I listen to a piece of music and say it's great, I have immediately created an opposite state. What we do if we are not trained in zen is to fall back again into some emotional expression of it. So we get an art critic looking at Cubism and saying it's fantastic. Rubbish. Cubism is, fantastic is something the critic makes of it.

It is against this background that I have chosen some poetry to try to show how zen is apparent in experience, in humour, in hope and in practice.

In experience, the choice is a piece of poetry from Wordsworth:

> *To sit without emotion, hope or aim, in the*
> *loved presence of my cottage fire*
> *and listen to the flapping of the flame or the*
> *kettle whispering its faint undersong.*

That is an experience.

In humour, this by an anonymous writer:

> *As I was going up the stair,*
> *I met a man who wasn't there,*
> *He wasn't there again today,*
> *I wish to God he'd go away.*

That's the humour of zen.

In hope, Tennyson's "Flower in a crannied wall":

> *If I could understand what you are,*
> *Root and all, and all in all,*
> *I should know what God and man is.*

Lastly, in practice, something by Alan Watts. Alan Watts was a great Buddhist writer, a great writer of zen:

> *In writing about Zen there are two extremes to be avoided. The one to define and explain so little that the reader is completely bewildered, and the other to define and explain so much that the reader thinks he understands Zen.*

So we have a state that exists that is unexplainable, that is unusable, has absolutely no value and is entirely useless, but explains everything. This is the strange paradox that we constantly come up against in our work. The paradox is my human mind constantly trying to come to terms with what it can't. To a mystic there is an unexplained situation that the mind constantly seeks to understand. If I didn't employ zen I would seek to explain it, and then I would have limited it to my explanation.

For me mysticism is an endless road of unending experience that evolves out of every moment. My relation to it simply is. It isn't right, it isn't wrong, it is how I survive. I can think of no better way of living because the sheer richness of my life is an experience of everything in every moment not reduced to my demand of it.

However, it is not marketable, nobody wants it. I say that with sadness because if you can relinquish your desire of life in the way that you think you should achieve it, there is nothing you will not be able to know. But paradoxically, there is nothing you will want to know.